BRAVE
NEW
HOME

BRAVE
NEW
HOME

Our Future in Smarter, Simpler, Happier Housing

DIANA LIND

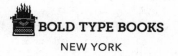

BOLD TYPE BOOKS

NEW YORK

Bold Type Books
116 East 16th Street, 8th Floor, New York, NY 10003
www.boldtypebooks.org
@BoldTypeBooks

Printed in the United States of America

First Edition: October 2020

Published by Bold Type Books, an imprint of Perseus Books, LLC, a subsidiary of Hachette Book Group, Inc. Bold Type Books is a co-publishing venture of the Type Media Center and Perseus Books.

The Hachette Speakers Bureau provides a wide range of authors for speaking events. To find out more, go to www.hachettespeakersbureau.com or call (866) 376-6591.

The publisher is not responsible for websites (or their content) that are not owned by the publisher.

Print book interior design by Six Red Marbles, Inc.

Library of Congress Cataloging-in-Publication Data

Names: Lind, Diana, author.
Title: Brave new home : our future in smarter, simpler, happier housing / Diana Lind.
Description: First edition. | New York : Bold Type Books, 2020. | Includes bibliographical references and index.
Identifiers: LCCN 2020020289 | ISBN 9781541742666 (hardcover) | ISBN 9781541742642 (ebook)
Subjects: LCSH: Housing—United States. | Housing, Single family—United States.
Classification: LCC HD7293 .L49 2020 | DDC 333.33/80973—dc23
LC record available at https://lccn.loc.gov/2020020289

ISBNs: 978-1-5417-4266-6 (hardcover), 978-1-5417-4264-2 (ebook)

LSC-C

10 9 8 7 6 5 4 3 2 1

To Greg

CONTENTS

INTRODUCTION

BEFORE BECOMING A MOM, I spent little time at home. I was always working, going out to dinner, hitting the gym, discovering new neighborhoods, spending evenings at cultural venues. But when my first son was born, just in time for winter in Philadelphia, that all changed. Now, with a (beautiful!) baby who needed constant feeding, diapering, and attention, I spent a lot of time in our row house. Instead of exploring the city, I explored my own mind, and my home. Before long, I felt uncharacteristically bored and isolated—even trapped.

When I became a parent, my world became centered around my house, and as a result, my values underwent an unexpected and dramatic transition. Suddenly, my husband and I were spending about an hour every day cooking and doing laundry, and another hour feeding, bathing, and cleaning up after our first son. We scrutinized our $300-per-month gas bill and spent our savings on home repairs. Things I thought I wanted in a home, such as a little extra space, had become just more rooms to clean and heat. Those early months with a newborn can be tough for anyone, but I couldn't help but wonder how humans had survived, and in such quantity, living this way—mostly alone, each family for itself.

But people hadn't always lived this way. This style of living, centered around the single-family home, is a relatively new concept in the history of humankind. Up until World War II, families traditionally lived in more communal situations, ranging from multigenerational households to close-knit neighborhoods full of friends and family. The things I'd yearned for during my maternity leave—other mothers to learn from, another family to have dinner with—were baked into living that way. Now my options were mommy-and-me classes at $20 a pop and family-friendly restaurants where kids watched YouTube on iPhones while their parents ate dinner.

Out of frustration with my living situation, and a lifelong fascination with cities and the built environment, I began to investigate housing choices in America and their economic, social, and environmental implications. For example, I drew a clear connection between the loneliness I experienced and the amount of time I spent at home. Did other Americans, new parents or not, share my sense of isolation at home? What were the economic and social consequences of people spending the bulk of their income on housing costs? What about the countless hours on household upkeep? How were various trends—like the country's rising housing costs, increasing social isolation, and decreasing fertility rate—related?

The more I researched these issues, the more I became convinced that the presumed benefits of single-family homes masked their negative social, economic, and environmental consequences. The data suggest that the current housing paradigm—predominantly oriented around owning a single-family home—is unaffordable, unhealthy, and out of step with consumer demand. And a large and growing portion of the population is unable to access the homeownership lifestyle, even if they desire it.

Housing affordability is a crisis, and not just in cities like New York and San Francisco; in Philadelphia, where I live, housing prices rose by 22 percent in a boom period between 2016 and mid-2017.[1] In Seattle, the median home price rose by $400,000 between 2012 and 2018.[2] The collision of high prices and limited supply is most acute in coastal cities, but it extends across the country. Utah, a state whose largest city has a little more than two hundred thousand people, created a Commission on Housing Affordability in 2018 to address the state's affordable housing gap. In desirable enclaves like Asheville, North Carolina, or Burlington, Vermont, monthly rental costs rival those of Miami and Boston, but average salaries don't.

Not surprisingly, the lack of housing choices and the prevalence of exclusionary housing regulations—such as minimum lot sizes and required off-street parking for each household—have made housing grow more expensive, decade over decade. Wages have not kept up with housing costs. In 1988, the typical sale price of a single-family home was 3.2 times the median household income. By 2017, the ratio was 4.2.[3] That same year, nearly thirty-eight million American households were "cost burdened," paying more than 30 percent of their income on rents and mortgages.[4]

Unaffordable housing is not just a problem for those struggling to pay off a mortgage or even for those who are locked out of homeownership and its financial upside. It is a societal problem. Studies show that the high cost of housing is driving widening inequality in the United States, serving as an obstacle to economic mobility, especially for young people and people of color. Homeownership divides the country along stark racial lines. In 1950, when 89.5 percent of Americans classified themselves as white, people of color were legally or extralegally prohibited from purchasing housing in many neighborhoods through redlining and restrictive covenants.[5] And now, when white Americans are trending toward minority status, only 44 percent of African Americans are homeowners, compared with 65.1 percent of all Americans and 73.7 percent of whites in the fourth quarter of 2019.[6] Not one of the one hundred cities with the largest black populations has closed this homeownership gap, and only three cities (Killeen, Texas; Fayetteville, North Carolina; and Charleston, South Carolina) have a gap of less than 20 percent.[7] To this day, the neighborhoods that were subject to redlining decades ago are still more prone to poverty. Given that homeownership is a significant means of growing wealth in this country, economic disparities between whites and people of color are inevitable.

Unaffordable housing also comes with serious mental and physical health ramifications. High housing costs often result in trade-offs, where families skimp on food and medical attention in order to pay the rent. An examination of the studies tracking the health effects of the 2008 foreclosure crisis found that experiencing a foreclosure—and even living near foreclosures— was associated with elevated levels of anxiety, depression, and violent behavior.[8] The Centers for Disease Control and Prevention (CDC) published a study looking at the link between the housing crisis from 2005 to 2010 and suicide. The study directly linked 1 to 2 percent of suicides to foreclosure and eviction.[9] The CDC report noted that some 68 percent of counselors working with clients to mitigate foreclosure found that "many" or "almost all" of their clients appeared depressed or hopeless.

There are also adverse health effects associated with sprawling, single-family suburbanization, including lower rates of walking and social interaction. While there may have once been an "urban health penalty" of a shorter life span, it hasn't applied for decades (when confounding factors such as race and income are controlled for). Today, life expectancy decreases as level of rurality increases.[10] Moreover, loneliness is becoming more common and being taken more seriously as a threat to physical and mental health. Studies have shown a link between loneliness and risk of stroke, high blood pressure, and cognitive decline. One study even suggested that loneliness is as lethal as smoking fifteen cigarettes a day.[11]

There are environmental consequences to single-family housing as well. At a time when the country is grappling with how to address the dangers of climate change and debating the possibility of a Green New Deal, the inefficiency of single-family homes can no longer be ignored. As American homes have become bigger, there have been a variety of environmental impacts: increased emissions from heating and cooling ever-larger private spaces; additional furniture for extra bedrooms, playrooms, and home offices; and additional appliances such as televisions and toilets. All this stuff has a carbon cost.

For all the presumed benefits of exclusion, privacy, and space that people experience in single-family homes, these economic, social, and environmental deficits are rarely mentioned. For so long, owning a single-family home has been seen as an unalloyed good, the American Dream. But changing demographics and cultural norms, along with the Great Recession's housing downturn and foreclosure crisis, and now COVID-19's economic uncertainties, are challenging how we balance the pros and cons of single-family homes.

There is a lot of discussion about our national malaise—one in eight Americans over age twelve has taken antidepressants—but we largely place the blame on the accelerating pace of life, distracting technology and media, and the downsides of globalization.[12] Why is so little attention paid to the home, the place where we spend the most time? And why isn't there a more robust public conversation about how living differently—more affordably, more communally, and more simply—could strengthen our society, economy, and health?

AT THE SAME time as the housing crisis has become acute, American demographics and social norms have shifted dramatically. Consider that at the turn of the twentieth century, most adults were married, a miniscule percentage were divorced, and the average family had 3.5 children.[13] This type of household strongly influenced the building boom following World War II, when the suburbs rapidly expanded and a new car-centric approach to living flourished.

Today, the prior dominance of white, heteronormative families has given way to a much more diverse country. According to analysis from the Brookings Institution, children under eighteen are already anticipated to be "majority minority" in 2020, with the whole country expected to be minority white by 2045.[14] The average age of first marriage has risen from early twenties in 1960 to late twenties today.[15] Marriage rates overall have dipped to their lowest levels since recording began in 1867, at just 6.5 marriages per one thousand people.[16] While the rate of divorce peaked in the 1990s, it's still between 40 and 50 percent.[17] Today's average family size is just 3.14 people, including children, and only 35 percent of home buyers have children under eighteen in the home.[18] Some 28 percent of Americans are now living alone.[19] Average life expectancy is near seventy-nine, having gained a decade in the past half century.[20] And these are just the demographics of today; imagine the world the next generation of Americans will inhabit. If trends continue, we should expect to see more people living alone, fewer new families (particularly among native-born Americans), further delay of marriage and more interracial marriages, and a population that skews older and older.

Americans' daily life and preferences have also changed, whether by choice or by force, to become more virtual, more mobile, and less stable. A society built around driving is looking for ways to incorporate a love of ride-hailing apps, electric scooters, and walkable neighborhoods. Our television habit has morphed into a phone addiction. Single-earner households have turned into dual-earner ones, and women now make up the majority of the college-educated workforce.[21] Steady jobs with daily commutes have declined, while the gig economy, working remotely, and even a rootless digital nomadism have taken hold. Freelancers currently make up 35 percent of the country's workforce and are expected to become the majority in the next decade.[22] Augmented reality and driverless cars are bound to shake up physical and social contours even more.

But housing today largely looks the same as it did in 1950. Granted, architecture has a certain permanence literally built in, but even brand-new developments are full of 2,500-square-foot houses with two-car garages. As so much of American life has changed, why hasn't housing?

I'd always assumed single-family homes were the way people wanted to live. We wouldn't have a country of culs-de-sac if people didn't really like them, right? But I found that the popularity of single-family living and homeownership writ large is only partly explained by choice. Government incentives, zoning, media narratives, advertising, and the housing industry all play a role in making single-family homes the de facto housing type in the United States.

Part One of this book explores how America transformed from a country of towns and cities where shared living, multipurpose buildings, and cheap temporary housing were very common to a country where single-family homes dominate.

The country's very beginning was rooted in small cities and towns, where people could fulfill their daily routines in a fifteen-minute walk. It would take centuries to get to the ideal of a white picket fence and detached home with a garage. Walt Whitman may have written that "a man is not a whole and complete man unless he owns a house and the ground it stands on," but for the first several decades following the country's independence, many Americans lived with extended family, hosted boarders, and rented rooms in a range of accommodations, from taverns to apartment hotels. Prior to the twentieth century, living alone as an adult man or woman was frowned upon, leading singletons to board with strangers or live with extended family to avoid stigma. And until privacy and space became the ultimate luxury, people lived relatively simply and densely.

Throughout all of these changes, the meaning of *home* evolved, from something more akin to shelter to an idealized vision of family life and a status symbol of achievement. This transformation, in turn, changed how people thought of residential neighborhoods, the good life, and how to raise families.

In some ways, the single-family home was a practical response to the desire for more space and access to nature. These homes, built for a nuclear or multigenerational family, had none of the transience or interaction with strangers that one might find in boardinghouses, the health problems that came with overcrowded communities, or the dirt and grime of an industrializing city. But for much of American history, building a single-family home away from the city was expensive and impractical.

A variety of technological and government innovations in the early twentieth century would change that. Some parts of cities had indeed become overcrowded. The densest parts of the Lower East Side of the late nineteenth century had housing densities comparable to contemporary Hong Kong, which has the benefit of residential skyscrapers to accommodate people. Both to ease the crowding and to facilitate suburban development, municipalities encouraged people to disperse to new communities once public trolleys and ferries could enable commuting.

Following World War I, a nationwide movement to support single-family homeownership sprang up. As construction methods became standardized, building homes became less expensive and less labor-intensive. By the end of World War II, modern lending practices, government-supported homeownership incentives, and the creation of a national highway network had forever changed the scale and location of housing in America.

The first half of the twentieth century also saw the birth and popularization of modern zoning codes that transformed what could be built and who could live where. In addition to making segregation essentially a permanent fixture of urban development in most cities through redlining and restrictive covenants, most zoning plans effectively made single-family homes the default. Multifamily housing, commercial, and industrial zones were restricted to limited, often lower-income, neighborhoods.

In addition, local governments and neighborhood associations promoted single-family homeownership as critical to creating clean and safe neighborhoods (even if the data didn't always bear this strategy out). Since renters tend to be from more racially diverse backgrounds and have lower wealth profiles, promoting homeownership has also been a strategy for local entities to skew whiter and wealthier without practicing overt or illegal discrimination.

All these factors help explain why contemporary housing has changed so little since that postwar boom era. Homeowners, developers, and local governments are deeply invested in maintaining the status quo. Homeowners are protective of what is often their greatest financial asset and investment, and use an array of mechanisms to discourage anything that could lower their property values. Multifamily housing, affordable housing, senior housing, student housing, and other alternatives all challenge the uniformity that is believed to prop up single-family housing prices.

For their part, real estate developers are risk averse and tend to build what has proven popular in the past. Besides that, building multifamily housing—especially anything outside the market-rate norm—is often exponentially more difficult to get through the gauntlet of neighborhood pushback and zoning variances.

Then there are the buyers and renters, who have been conditioned to seek out the maximum amount of space they can afford. Not until the recent and increasingly dire affordability crisis did the growing demographic of people living alone demand more micro-apartments, tiny homes, and shared living options.

But much has changed in the twenty-first century that makes old development patterns and lifestyles untenable. The Great Recession in 2008 shook many people's fundamental belief in the safety of real estate investments; it also devastated many people's finances, threatening their ability to remain or become homeowners. Likewise, as cities with highly concentrated job markets and lagging construction—like Washington, DC, and San Francisco—have become beleaguered by escalating housing costs, crushing traffic, and gentrification, they've exposed just how inefficient and expensive single-family living is. As people seek refuge from flooding and fires as our planet warms, new housing options are sorely needed. And as a new generation comes of age with different expectations and needs, housing will have to become less expensive and isolating and more sustainable, shared, and accessible to their daily routines.

This confluence of factors—housing unaffordability, a more demographically diverse population, environmental concerns, and dissatisfaction with the single-family home—is galvanizing an unlikely coalition of priced-out would-be homeowners, architects and developers, affordable housing advocates, Silicon Valley entrepreneurs, and progressive politicians who are pushing for brave new forms of housing and policies that can encourage their adoption.

In Part Two of the book, I will share stories of how individuals, companies, and governments are beginning to reflect this need for change. What's old is new again: reinterpretations of single-room-occupancy buildings are popping up in cities, in the form of both hip co-living communities and workforce housing for teachers and service professionals.

Co-living has grown popular because it meets several needs that single-family homes don't: more socialization, less consumer friction in everything from utility accounts to furniture, and the convenience of all-inclusive fees and shorter leases. Some providers differentiate themselves by offering smart, eco-friendly interior design, in-house yoga or cooking classes, and off-site visits to go wine tasting or skiing.

Recognizing demand, governments are finding ways to encourage co-living, particularly for those who can't afford the all-inclusive kind. Atlanta's largest co-living community, built in partnership with co-living developer Common, will include affordable housing among its 345 beds. New York City's Department of Housing Preservation and Development created an initiative to explore shared housing typologies that can demonstrate to the public and developers the potential for affordable communal living, and how zoning and other regulations will be adapted for it. For its first pilot, the ShareNYC initiative will create or preserve approximately three hundred housing "opportunities"—a new term for co-living units or beds. As governments and co-living operators destigmatize shared living, the market may follow with more housing that works for different budgets.

Co-living is getting plenty of headlines, but it's not the only alternative to the single-family home. Micro-apartments and tiny houses are also attractive to the 28 percent of the population living alone, who are often looking for inexpensive, manageable housing options. More and more developers are creating micro-apartment buildings and tiny-home communities for workforce housing: teachers, service-industry workers, even tech workers. For example, a school district outside of Tucson is investing $200,000 in infrastructure improvements to create a tiny-home community to house its teachers. Tiny homes are becoming affordable enough—the global nonprofit New Story has partnered with Austin company ICON to 3D print a 650-square-foot house at a cost of just $10,000—that city governments from Seattle to Detroit are employing them as a solution to the affordable housing and homelessness crises.

Still, these housing styles often face legal challenges where zoning requires that units be a certain size—often no smaller than three hundred square feet—or have certain characteristics, such as a seemingly arbitrary length of kitchen countertop. One has to wonder how much more popular these forms of housing would be if they could be legally built in the majority of residential neighborhoods, or if there wasn't stigma, rooted in classism, associated with mobile homes.

Tiny houses are becoming popular not only as primary residences, but as accessory dwelling units (ADUs). ADUs have long been called granny flats, in-law units, and backyard cottages, but were long discouraged in places like the sprawling suburbs of California, where minimum house and lot sizes are sacred. But new legislation in that state at the end of 2016 clarified how and where ADUs can be built, and housing and community development departments are promoting their many benefits: affordability, allowing for extended family to live closely with privacy, and creating additional income via rental.[23]

ADUs have found friends—and plenty of enemies too—in many of the country's metropolitan areas, like Minneapolis and Portland, where a lack of residential density is thwarting the aspirations of denser, more transit-oriented neighborhoods. ADUs provide more than just housing: they're a way to achieve a density that can support transit and a stronger tax base. Some local governments are promoting ADUs as a compromise: a way to grow the city's population and housing stock without fundamentally altering the suburban character of its neighborhoods. In Philadelphia, the city recently approved ADUs on historic properties as a way to encourage owners to maintain the character of historic, and often underinvested, residential neighborhoods.

ADUs are also tech compatible. As 3D printing, prefabrication, and modular and inexpensive customization make housing production accessible to the masses, ordering a home online could soon be as easy as ordering clothes. Venture capitalists, technologists, and entrepreneurial architects are looking at ways to change the typical development model. Instead of always building on spec, where risk-averse developers must cater to a family of four, what if builders could cheaply tailor plans to suit less conventional demands? As these technologies evolve and expand, they could lower housing prices and speed up construction.

A lack of customized housing is a key issue for one growing sector of the market: multigenerational families. Latino, Asian, and black families have long traditions of living with extended family, and these groups are growing as a proportion of the overall population. Due to them, and to a growing number of white families who moved in together for economic reasons, multigenerational living is at its highest point since 1950. Pew Research Center found that in 2016 20 percent of Americans, or sixty-four million people, lived multigenerationally. Families of all kinds are enjoying the benefits of sharing resources and having extra capacity to care for young children or elderly grandparents.

As baby boomers retire and look to downsize or reduce their housing costs, many aren't interested in living in traditional fifty-five-plus communities. Instead, they want to age in place, with some families opting to do so through multigenerational housing. By living with younger kin, seniors can provide and receive informal support while reducing housing costs. Major developers like Pardee Homes and Lennar are also starting to build models geared toward multigenerational families, featuring in-law suites with separate entrances or distinct wings of a house for different sets of family members. While they sound like small alterations, these changes are effectively challenging the ideal of an independent single-family home. And developers are seeing that there's a market for multigenerational homes and that building them could prove profitable.

Multigenerational housing is encouraged in some countries, like Singapore and Germany, because of its health benefits to seniors. Here, developers are taking a different approach to improving health outcomes through housing. The social determinants of health are considered to have an enormous impact on a person's well-being. Up to 40 percent of health outcomes can be traced to nonmedical issues like housing, income, and access to healthy food.[24]

Hospitals, governments, and developers are becoming attuned to the biggest medical spenders—such as the homeless, the addicted, and the elderly—and finding novel ways to house them. In New Jersey, a statewide financial institution is helping hospitals build housing for homeless people, the most frequent users of emergency rooms and, therefore, the most expensive users of the hospital system. Hospitals like the Mayo Clinic, based in Rochester, Minnesota, are investing in public-private economic development to transform their surrounding community into a healthier one.

The aging of the American population will also determine how health and housing intersect. In 2050, there will be more than eighty-three million seniors, almost double the forty-three million seniors counted in 2012.[25] The single-family home embodies financial and social independence, but nowadays, health-care amenities and services are the cutting edge of holistic housing.

Meanwhile, the wellness trend is encroaching on housing and garnering attention from people who want to grow their own food, breathe cleaner air, live less sedentary lifestyles, and escape the chaos of modern life. While in the past, people wanted to live on a golf course and dine at the clubhouse, today's communities, which may not be any less exclusionary, are nonetheless marketed toward people who want to spend their spare time gardening in communal plots and sharing their bounty with neighbors.

All of these kinds of housing reflect a frustration with the high costs, unhealthiness, injustice, and inconvenience of current housing options. But single-family homes didn't become the norm organically, and these new housing types won't break through to the mainstream simply through market demand. How can people get the housing they deserve? How can we ensure that all people can benefit from the twenty-first-century disruption of the status quo?

In Part Three of the book, we'll examine the ways that our government, as well as the media and private sector, can take this momentum forward.

Today, everything from dating to currency has gone digital; fewer people can afford homes; inclusivity and antidiscrimination policies are essential; and millennials reject ownership models and expect instability. In this environment, housing is bound to change. For the sake of our society, it has to.

Governments at the state and local levels are finally hearing the message. In a striking range of states, from Oregon to Virginia to Nebraska, policymakers are questioning single-family zoning and proposing banning it everywhere, with the exception of small towns. Local leaders from New York City to Austin are encouraging ADUs and shared-housing models. Officials at all levels are reexamining policies, such as the mortgage interest deduction, which have for so long given advantages to the wealthy.

But changing housing incrementally will not work in the twenty-first century. Ultimately, to rethink housing will require dissecting and fundamentally challenging a number of assumptions. For example, we have long assumed that homeownership is a net positive, both for individuals and for municipalities. It's time we questioned how much of that has to do with homeownership in and of itself and how much with the savings, patient capital, and low interest rates embedded in thirty-year mortgages. If the two were separated, could there be other wealth-creation opportunities that might be better suited to contemporary lifestyles and the problems that come with them? What about opportunities like community land trusts and other shared equity models, which could help make housing more permanently affordable and help neighbors share in the upside?

In the private sector, among developers, architects, and banks, there is increasing recognition that for all the privacy and independence single-family living affords, it is a lifestyle with significant costs. Each household maintains its own dwelling, makes its own meals, and transports its own way to work and school. Each household pays for its own internet and television connection, its own entertainment and news. Each household has its own heating and cooling system, washer and dryer, plumbing, and appliances. Developers are beginning to rethink this model. Architects and furniture designers are contemplating how to make homes flexible enough to accommodate different kinds of users over the course of their lifetimes. Banks are looking at new financial products to meet the growing demand for ADUs and other structures typically outside a thirty-year mortgage. Venture capital funds, seeing an industry ripe for disruption, are beginning to deploy more money toward housing innovation. Vigilance on the part of the government and media is necessary to ensure that these new ventures allow residents to share in the upside.

Up to now, stories of alternatives to single-family homes have generally been underreported, or even misreported. Reporters often demean co-living with snarky allusions to "adult dorms." (It is hard to imagine such a cynical viewpoint coming from media in, say, Europe, where social connection is seen as essential to life, rather than a bourgeois fad.) These articles rarely account for the tyranny of single-family living and the way it has diminished the availability of different affordable, social, or convenient housing choices for all Americans. By treating alternatives to the current model of housing as somehow abnormal, they underestimate the true demand for innovative housing products.

But there is also a vibrant debate happening, mostly via social media and predominantly on Twitter, where discussions about the minutiae of legislation, a new development, or a piece of research can result in hundreds of comments. This community hints at the untapped audience hungry for real discussion about today's housing crises and solutions. It represents the passion of individuals to tackle the housing problem for themselves. Self-identified YIMBYs (for "yes in my backyard," meaning people who encourage development) have succeeded in lobbying for dense development in housing-starved areas. Even on the smallest scale, as people throughout this book demonstrate, individuals who choose to open their homes and their backyards to tenants and ADUs are having an impact.

What follows is a guide to housing in the twenty-first century—the context of today's housing challenges, the stories of new housing solutions, and a road map for the difficult but necessary journey our society must bravely undertake. Once you see how America fell in love with the single-family home and why it has fallen out, you will never see your own home the same way again.

A HISTORY OF SINGLE-FAMILY HOUSING

CHAPTER ONE

THE GOLDEN AGE
OF SHARED LIVING

TODAY, THE STANDALONE HOME with its white picket fence is the emblem of the American Dream. But this style of habitation was hardly typical when the country was first born. Back then, Americans rarely lived without kin, servants, apprentices, boarders, or enslaved people. A minority of people owned their homes and few bought houses with large mortgages. Most people lived in small cities where housing was located in walking distance to, if not directly above or alongside, commercial activity. In other words, current housing norms were once pretty unusual.

At the very beginning of the colonies, housing was as rough-and-tumble as the original settlers. While houses at the time tended to be crowded and dirty—with dirt floors and all—being indoors was still preferable to being outdoors. For colonists, the backyard had yet to become the bucolic, tame experience that we romanticize today. Rather, nature meant danger and uncertainty, and houses prioritized protection against the elements over aesthetics.

Initially, towns were populated with what might look like tiny homes today—hastily constructed, single-room huts framed in timber that were rudimentary even by the standards of the home-lands the colonists had left behind.[1] In these early towns, housing was only as big as a family needed or could afford to heat. Families could sleep in the warm upper lofts of a one- or two-story home, and so as a family needed more space, they expanded upward. Houses sprawled horizontally only to accommodate uninsulated outbuildings, kitchens, and quarters for enslaved people or servants.

While some families built their own houses, many single men, travelers, and sailors lived at inns or as boarders in private homes. This was a time of great geographic mobility, making temporary housing more convenient to men who moved as needed to pursue professional opportunities. Taverns and inns also had the benefit of built-in company in the form of fellow travelers and innkeepers. When the Boston tavern The King's Arms was sold in 1650, its inventory offered a glimpse of the way that food, entertainment, and lodging were all mixed at the time. The tavern's ground floor had a grand room called the "Exchange," a kitchen and pantry, and a parlor. Upstairs were the rooms for rent for the "better sort of people," including space for a nursery. For regular folks, there was a garret divided into three small sleeping compartments. The yard consisted of a brewery, stable, five hog sties, and one "house of office."[2]

This image of a bustling building that combined multiple uses—tavern, inn, brewhouse, office, and animal habitat—also illustrates the way early American towns grew: organically, and without any official zoning. In a time before cars, it was im-practical to separate commercial and residential (not to mention agricultural) activities across large distances. With the horse-drawn carriage as the primary mode of land transportation, housing had to be in close proximity to amenities. Housing and work were intertwined: people often lived above or alongside where they worked, and tradespeople often offered free housing to apprentices as part of their compensation. Even after factories became commonplace in the nineteenth century, many artisans lived adjacent to the shops where they produced their goods.[3]

These early towns also lacked the capacity or interest to heavily regulate what went on in and around housing. In 1637, Dutch governor Willem Kieft took a census of New Amsterdam (now New York), only to find that one-quarter of houses were "grog-shops." Lines blurred between housing and inn, and between inn and bar. (While people today don't typically crave in-home breweries, neighborhoods that provide housing with quick access to restaurants and bars tend to be popular.)

With little private, clean, or quiet space indoors, people spent much of their time out of their houses and in the streets, which consequently were full of activity. Life was crowded, both within the house and within the town. In a far cry from the levels of privacy we experience today, house and street were interconnected; people could hear the street indoors, and the private lives of families could just as easily be heard on the street.

While there was still a quiet, rural fringe often just a mile or so from the center of town, the major cities such as New York, Boston, and Philadelphia soon became more compact, ever more centered around the commercial core. By the 1700s, houses in these cities were often no longer built as standalone structures, but rather with a "toothing" at the party wall that assumed another building would soon adjoin it.[4] Attached housing not only kept the city as compact as possible, and, therefore, as easily traversed by foot or carriage as possible, but also gave each home more insulation against the elements.

A visitor to Philadelphia in 1698 described the city's common row houses as "most of them stately, and of brick, generally three stories high, after the mode in London, and as many as several families in each."[5] By the mid-eighteenth century, overcrowding was a problem in cities, despite considerable new and ongoing construction. Siblings often shared beds, and sometimes whole families crammed into one bed. Lots were subdivided, and multifamily and multistory buildings soon became more prevalent.

Although the colonies were on the cusp of forming a new country, where an entrepreneurial spirit would guide growth for centuries to come, colonial society was still very much like its European counterpart, with a large base of low-income people and a few very wealthy people. Author Keith Krawczynski's book *Daily Life in the Colonial City* provides some of the data illustrating inequality in cities at the time. He notes that in late colonial Philadelphia, 80 percent of heads of household did not own their homes, and the wealthiest 10 percent of Philadelphians owned 70 percent of the city's real estate and collected 90 percent of the rents.[6]

Early Americans viewed housing quite differently than we do today. There was little expectation of privacy, stability, ownership, or regulations, all of which are cornerstones of contemporary real estate. Back then, housing was simply shelter. The ways we commonly think of a home—a place of refuge, a backyard meant for leisure, a private space for the nuclear family— were not yet in play.[7]

THE PHYSICAL ATTRIBUTES and sociological meaning attributed to housing began to change in the nineteenth century—a time when just about everything was changing. At the time of its independence, the United States had been a predominantly rural country with pockets of population in a handful of East Coast cities. At the 1800 Census, the population was 94 percent rural, but by 1900 it would be 60 percent (by contrast, it is just 15 percent today).[8] New York and Philadelphia, the country's two largest cities at the dawn of the nineteenth century, had only a little more than one hundred thousand people between them.[9] While the Louisiana Purchase in 1803 extended the country's territory as far west as Montana, most of the population still lived east of the Mississippi. But this sleepy patchwork of urban development would quickly change in the coming decades. Housing would have to change as a result.

During the nineteenth century, the United States grew at a clip of more than 30 percent each decade, with most of that growth coming to cities. The country's total population would expand from just five million in 1800 to seventy-five million in 1900. It was an astounding flourishing of people, due to a combination of natural population growth, growing immigration (more than twenty-seven million would immigrate to the country between 1880 and 1930), and the slave trade, which would eventually bring more than three hundred thousand people to the country against their will.[10] In the nineteenth century, not only would the scale of population grow explosively, but the country's dominant economic activity would shift from agriculture to industry, changing how cities and the countryside were connected.

Amid this frenzy of growth, expansion, and economic activity, people arrived in cities to build their lives and make their fortunes. Housing had to be dense and cheap to enable cities to absorb thousands of new residents each week and mitigate extreme housing price appreciation. As the population grew exponentially, so did housing.

By the mid-1800s, urban housing, whether a Philadelphia row house or a San Francisco Victorian, tended to be larger, an indication both of growing affluence of homeowners and of improved building technology. These more spacious homes, ranging up to 3,500 square feet, enabled extended families to live together more comfortably. And because families were occupying more space than they needed, they could sublease to boarders when necessary.

The row houses, brownstones, and townhomes that lined cities from Boston down to Baltimore were flexible structures that could be divided into multiple units or boardinghouses as needed. Boardinghouse historian Wendy Gamber estimates that "between one-third and one-half of nineteenth-century urban residents either took in boarders or were boarders themselves."[11] While full-fledged boardinghouses became popular in the 1800s, there were also many families that welcomed occasional boarders, much like contemporary Airbnb hosts.

If the expansive size of new homes explains boarding on the supply side, a multitude of factors explain the appeal of boarding on the demand side. Many boarders had recently arrived in a new place knowing few people and with little money on hand. Boarding was often cheaper and faster than long-term renting or owning. Additionally, society stigmatized living entirely alone, leading bachelors and widows to seek housing with families. As a result of these and other factors, less than 3 percent of adults lived alone in 1890, compared with 28 percent of Americans today.

Today, a person who lives in a motel would likely be thought of as "housing insecure," but back then living in a boardinghouse or other transient accommodation was often a normal first step in moving to a new city. Economic mobility was high (especially compared to society today), so it was not unusual for a person to move to a city, live in a boardinghouse, and later become a property owner.

For example, when Benjamin Franklin first arrived in Philadelphia, he was "penniless" and stayed at a boardinghouse along Market Street. After he married his wife Deborah, they spent decades renting homes throughout the city.[12] Only after a number of years in Philadelphia did he eventually build his own home. But true to the times and Franklin's entrepreneurial roots, it was a mixed-use building with a print shop, bindery, and foundry, as well as two rental properties.

There was little distinction between boarder and host in financial terms. People often took in others in times of economic need, and families who took in the occasional lodger did not think of themselves as running boardinghouses.[13] Lodging got intimate quickly: travelers to inns and taverns could expect to share not only a room with a stranger, but even a bed. Much like sailors and bedmates Ishmael and Queequeg in the famous midcentury novel *Moby Dick*, many young men made friends through boarding together.

Boardinghouse life was not always rosy. A veteran landlady interviewed by the *New York Times* in November 1889 pronounced boardinghouse keeping "the most cruel and thankless way a woman can earn her living." Her grievances included "Weary days and sleepless, anxious nights," suspicious landlords, and boarders who treated her "as if she were a sort of an upper servant."[14] Numerous cartoons of the period depicted the women who ran boardinghouses as wretched misers who took advantage of people.

Amid all the social and technological change in the nineteenth century, boarding eventually became "the bête noire of mid-century moralists," historian Wendy Gamber says in *The Boardinghouse in Nineteenth-Century America*. Instead of viewing boardinghouses as value neutral—a living situation that had its share of benefits and problems—Americans soon saw them as the antithesis to wholesome domestic life.

The uneasiness surrounding boardinghouses came at a time when housing became a home, laden with symbolism and meaning. Boardinghouses were the antithesis of the wholesome nuclear family and the single-family home that went with it. In boardinghouses, domestic comfort was furnished out of a financial incentive, not love; family and strangers interacted, often without clear protocol. Gamber notes, "In an era dominated by powerful—if often illusory—dichotomies between home and market, public and private, love and money, boardinghouses emerged as unsavory counterparts to idealized homes. Or, to put it another way, they offered nineteenth-century Americans a means of defining home by representing everything that home was not."[15]

Today, we still grapple with issues that muddy the meaning of home. House flippers frustrate the ideal of earnest, family home buyers. Commodified community in co-living irks some as an inauthentic way of building friendships. But the home has never truly been free of market demands.

BY THE LATE nineteenth century, the transience that was once commonplace and in fact necessary slowly gave way to two classes of people: newcomers and the establishment. With many of the newcomers being immigrants—often from Ireland, Italy, and eastern Europe—the blurry boundaries between host and boarder, between newcomer and established resident, became more fixed in order to enforce class and ethnic differences. At the same time, boardinghouses and overcrowded apartments were meeting increased opposition from reformers and local governments. Gone were the days when you could have a hog sty in your backyard without anyone caring!

At the same time, as in-home servants became less prevalent and slavery was abolished, it became more of a norm for the household to be limited to the nuclear family. Families themselves were quickly becoming smaller: the average American family had slightly more than five children in 1870, but an average of four children just two decades later in 1890.

Alongside population growth and changing norms, housing and development also adjusted to new technology. The creation of the railroad system, the emergence of trolleys, and the proliferation of private automobiles changed the geography of whole metropolitan areas. Following the Civil War, land speculation was rampant. And as mass-produced steel enabled the construction of larger and taller buildings, developers focused on high-density housing as a way to maximize profit on land.

In this context, a new hybrid emerged, encompassing the hominess of a boardinghouse and the commercial atmosphere of a hotel: the apartment hotel. The apartment hotel took the boardinghouse's advantages (short-term room and board) and tried to mitigate its disadvantages (the professional inefficiencies and personal awkwardness of the small scale). Tremont House, built in Boston in 1829, is noted as the first hotel to have indoor plumbing and bathrooms, bellboys, and free soap. Novelist Charles Dickens wrote about it in his travelogue, *American Notes*, saying, "The hotel (a very excellent one)...has more galleries, colonnades, piazzas, and passages than I can remember, or the reader would believe."[16]

This style of residential hotel was imitated and proliferated throughout the nineteenth and early twentieth century. While these hotels catered to short-term stays, they also became semipermanent forms of residence. Some featured gendersegregated dining rooms and parlors, provided amenities such as laundry and libraries that prefigure today's co-living common spaces, and allowed a degree of anonymity that the intimacy of the boardinghouse could not offer.

Apartment hotels were not just for bachelors and bachelorettes; families enjoyed them as well. In Columbia University professor Gwendolyn Wright's history of American housing, *Building the Dream*, she notes that wealthy families were attracted to apartment hotels' convenience and technological advantages. "Some saw [the apartment houses] as utopian settings: auguring a cooperative society, providing technological precision and infinitely available comforts." Rather than move to the privatism in the suburbs, some families preferred the communal and creative apartment hotel and its perch in the city.[17]

In a way, some apartment hotels prefigured Uber Eats and some of the amenity-laden condos and co-living arrangements of today. An 1871 apartment hotel on lower Fifth Avenue in New York featured public dining rooms and laundry service. Residents could eat in an elegant dining room on the first floor or have their food brought up to them.[18] Wright explains, "For rents ranging between $650 and $2,200 a year…it was possible to do away with many of the smells, sounds, and wasted space of household drudgery."

For those who couldn't afford an apartment house, many found space in a much less chic type of multistory building that prevailed during this time: the tenement. Tenements, which were once synonymous with any multifamily dwelling, became a distinct housing type in the late 1800s. They were often called railroad tenement apartments, because they were designed without hallways and one passed through the apartment, room by room, as one does through a train's cars. These tenements succeeded in housing tremendous numbers of people, but did so by sacrificing adequate access to air and light. It may have been that crowded urban housing conditions merely correlated with disease rather than caused it (after all, rural areas with sewage problems and malnourished workers also cultivated disease), but tenements would become associated with a myriad of controversial issues such as poor health, overwork, and poverty. If the boardinghouse seemed problematic in the middle of the nineteenth century, the tenement was, by the end of the century, an official crisis.

In this period following the Civil War, public health took on a new sense of urgency. After thousands of soldiers died unnecessarily due to unsanitary conditions in war camps, the public health reform movement took on a variety of health issues—including crowded housing—through new zoning regulations.

Zoning came to be seen as a tool that could protect people's well-being. But it was also used to punish and segregate immigrants. In San Francisco, legislators passed the Cubic Air Ordinance in 1870, which required five hundred cubic feet of air per occupant. While such a law would indeed promote better living conditions, it also resulted in hundreds of arrests, primarily of Chinese immigrants whose apartments were then later occupied by white residents.[19]

In New York, legislation in 1879 similarly required that every room in a tenement have access to fresh air. Tenements built after this law passed were called dumbbell tenements, because they narrowed in the middle to create air shafts that allowed for a tiny bit of light and air and maintained the maximum square footage for living space. That tenements rather easily flouted existing zoning codes made it all the more urgent that cities develop stricter requirements to bring them under control. A New York City law governing tenements that passed in 1901 provided more extensive rules for waste disposal, indoor plumbing, outdoor courtyards, and access to fresh air. It essentially established the modern zoning code that would guide the city's development for a century.

In the years between these two laws, Jacob Riis's 1890 book, *How the Other Half Lives*, was published. Riis's book, which used shocking, candid photography and impassioned storytelling to document the squalor of tenement life, became an immediate best seller that reformers and regular citizens alike marshaled to condemn tenements. But while Riis's work would have a major impact on society, and is to this day the most commonly cited source on the problem of urban overcrowding, it was merely part of a chorus of media about the problems with urban living. As newspapers published frequent reports about hazardous tenement conditions, even luxury multifamily buildings became tainted by their association with density.[20]

Reformers also undertook the cause of children mistreated at home, school, or work. City life and shared living were demonized for their purported contributions to the problems of children's unhappiness and overwork. The *Child Welfare Manual* criticized raising a family in the city, declaring, "It is hard to think of a real home stored in diminutive pigeon-holes.... The quarters are so crowded that not only is it necessary to use folding Christmas-trees, but the natural, free intercourse of the family is crowded out; there is no room to play, no place for reading-room and music and hearth-side; and so families fold up their affections too."[21] For many families, this kind of anti-urban-living commentary was powerful enough to encourage them to seek, literally, greener pastures and more spacious homes. Suburbia would gain in popularity not only because of its advantageous privacy and greenery, but because of the fear that narratives like this instilled in parents. Raising kids in the city became essentially synonymous with neglect.

RIIS'S WORK ARRIVED just as electric streetcars transformed where people could live and work within a city. When Riis was writing about the Lower East Side, the population density had peaked at more than four hundred thousand people per square mile—comparable to the kind of dense habitation prevalent in today's Hong Kong or Manila, where people live in skyscrapers and not in five-story tenements.[22] Streetcars helped ease this kind of crowding by allowing for urban expansion into the early suburbs, which were often within a short distance of the city's core. Indeed, part of Riis's prescription for ameliorating tenements was to encourage people to move out of the city. Low-cost fares and free transfers encouraged city dwellers to live outside densely inhabited areas and commute into the city for work.

This new suburban sprawl was fast and had a tremendous domino effect. Robert Bruegmann, author of one of the defining books on the topic, *Sprawl*, captures the quick exodus from the city:

After several decades of outward movement, there were not enough tenants left to fill the oldest and least sanitary tenements on the Lower East Side. In response to the outward migration, together with new, tighter building laws, many building owners boarded up their properties above the first floor or abandoned them altogether. Densities plummeted. Manufacturing firms dispersed along with the residents, sometimes in advance and sometimes trailing, as they required larger and more up-to-date facilities. Along with the factories, many retail establishments dispersed as well. Both the residential and the employment density curves in the New York area flattened rapidly.[23]

As the demographics of who lived in cities radically changed, the location of jobs diversified, and streetcar technology allowed for a more dispersed metropolis, housing underwent a shift from urban to suburban, shared to private, rented to owned. And although there was never a halcyon period of American inclusive diversity, during this era of exodus cities and suburbs grew more segregated by race and class.

With jobs moving out of the city center and dense housing viewed negatively, many of the old forms of housing came under attack because of how they purportedly affected people's moral character. The legitimate concern about overcrowded housing as a public health issue slowly morphed into unproven ideas that densely populated housing would have negative mental and even physical consequences. Despite there being a wide range of living situations between overcrowded tenements and single-family homes, there was little room for nuance. Suburbia was always depicted as uplifting.

At the same time that late nineteenth-century and early twentieth-century urban buildings, whether tenements or apartment hotels or plain apartment buildings, made little appeal to the symbolic concept of the home, new model cottages in the suburbs developed a novel narrative for housing. Early streetcar suburbs often offered larger and more private homes than those found in the core city. In places like West Philadelphia, Mount Lebanon in Pittsburgh, and Mount Pleasant in Washington, DC, the turn-of-the-century homes looked like English-style country cottages with stone cladding and landscaped yards. These houses illustrate the true ambitions of suburban and rural architecture—not only to escape overcrowding, but to emulate the rich.

American aesthetics were evolving. Victorian architecture in the late nineteenth and twentieth century demonstrated a preoccupation with nature, personal expression, and family life. In the 1920s, when advertisements, media, and literature all promoted national parks and resort hotels to the middle class, the benefits of outdoor life, fresh air, and exercise became codified as part of American family life. Soon, the image of the suburban home and its inherent domesticity, access to nature, and the "good family" became interchangeable concepts. Even if people still living in the tenements aspired to this lifestyle, it was out of their price range.

When people didn't willingly move out of dense urban areas, they were often pushed out. Under the banner of noblesse oblige and public health concern, city governments authorized slum clearance—the practice of demolishing substandard buildings and replacing them with new development. By the early twentieth century, tenements were being razed because of their high rates of contagious diseases. In one drastic example in 1905, Chicago cleared two hundred buildings within a two-block area and displaced some 3,500 people.[24] Although building owners were compensated for their loss, tenants often had no recourse.

WHILE THE RISE of the single-family home was supported by many factors at the turn of the twentieth century—a public health movement that was biased against the density of urban life, a family-centric approach to living, the creation of street-car transit, and the incentivizing of early suburbia—its near-complete dominance of housing was not yet a given.

A variety of housing choices sprung up at the time to offer alternatives to the binary of tenements or single-family homes: Companies built entire communities for their workers. Cooperatives of workers built their own housing projects. Women's empowerment groups created women-run and lived-in communities, like YWCAs and housing for female professionals. Before city governments paid to build subsidized housing, local philanthropists stepped in to build model tenements with more access to shared outdoor areas.

But the strategies employed to improve tenements hint at the difficulty of bridging these housing types with the growing paradigm of familial privacy. Model tenements moved social activity into central courtyards and off the streets, in effect moving public life into the private realm. Eventually, public concern that shared indoor space encouraged unsavory behavior (because it allowed people of different ages, backgrounds, and families to mix) extended to shared outdoor space. The only palatable option, then, was a private home with a private backyard.

For a brief period at the beginning of the twentieth century, dense housing types and suburbia coexisted, but by the 1920s it was clear that cities were losing out to suburbs. In that decade, the suburbs grew twice as quickly as core cities.[25]

The houses of the era were typically modest but technologically modern. Single-family homes had their own plumbing and heating, neither of which came cheap. The rambling houses of the Victorian era gave way to small Capes and Craftsman houses that no longer featured extra rooms like libraries or spare bedrooms. The interior decoration style of white ethnic immigrants—often ornate and full of mementos—was now met with the simplicity of modernism, which claimed a superior aesthetic on moral grounds but was equally a way for its proponents to differentiate themselves from the lower classes.

There were some feminist implications to smaller, simpler houses with appliances, like washing machines and dishwashers, that could save women from time toiling on domestic tasks. That said, the single-family home's emphasis on an idealized domestic sphere drew ire from women. *Harper's Bazaar* magazine called the single-family home "a prison and a burden and a tyrant."[26] Charlotte Perkins Gilman campaigned against the isolating, demanding domestic ideal. Her vision for residential architecture, which was remarkable for its time, was one that freed women of their responsibilities to the home. Her ideas of cooperatives for housewives, community dining halls, kitchen-less houses, and publicly funded day care would fit right into today's reimaginations of housing.

All of this would come to a head with the end of World War I. The country was demoralized and shaken by a war that had slaughtered millions of people and resulted in a tenuous peace. The country's economy was also in a slump. As the government sought to intervene in support of economic growth and also boost morale, housing became the perfect vehicle to accomplish these goals simultaneously.

CHAPTER TWO

THE RISE OF THE
SINGLE-FAMILY HOME

I N THE 1920S, PEOPLE around the globe were grappling with the aftermath of World War I. The war had destroyed the old world order and cracked open a Pandora's box of modernity. The breakthrough advances in technology and changing social mores enabled by the war forecast a transformative modern era: women were fighting for the vote, private automobiles now proliferated in cities, manufacturing was bringing goods like clothing and furniture more cheaply to the masses, and skyscrapers embodied the almost limitless ambition of American society. At the same time, the postwar economy seesawed between boom and bust.

The city's physical makeup was shifting dramatically—in part due to zoning regulations, but also because cars had become more widely available and affordable. As cars became a must-have for the middle class, car companies, in conjunction with local governments, began dismantling public transportation to better accommodate cars in the streets. Most famously, the likes of General Motors, Firestone Tires, Standard Oil of California, and Phillips Petroleum funded holding companies called National City Lines and Pacific City Lines to buy up trolley networks across the country. They subsequently put the trolley lines out of business and replaced them with buses, which didn't require dedicated tracks and could share the road with cars. Railroad companies, some of the most profitable enterprises civilization had ever known, started to consolidate and slowly go out of business.

Cars enabled people to decouple where they lived and worked, radically changing personal mobility and resulting in new patterns of development. Cities now had the luxury of defining distinct districts for manufacturing, residential, commercial, and other purposes. All of these changes further encouraged single-family housing development over multipurpose buildings in cities. Mixed-use buildings with retail at street level and residential above, which had been the cornerstone of nineteenth-century urban life, would become rarer in the twentieth.

The proliferation of private cars also allowed for more dispersed metropolitan areas, spawning urban-planning visions of de-densified cities that fully accommodated cars. In the early twentieth century, many American cities joined the City Beautiful movement—an urban-planning fad that like England's garden city style espoused the role of grand, formal landscape design and monumental architecture to uplift people. The movement sought to connect urbanites to parks and open spaces to increase their personal well-being, but it often did so by demolishing existing residential neighborhoods. City Beautiful efforts in cities like Philadelphia, Washington, DC, Chicago, and Cleveland resulted in heavy doses of grandeur, such as a copy of the Champs-Élysées that cut diagonally across Philadelphia's dense, grid-bound city with six lanes of traffic and allées of trees. Washington, DC, adopted a new comprehensive plan to provide grand vistas of its monuments. Cleveland sought to build a central mall with Beaux Arts buildings around it. Lanes of car traffic always accompanied these monumental designs, as if in celebration of modernity and urban pomp.

Shortly after the City Beautiful efforts took hold, architects like Le Corbusier drew up radical plans to reform cities for the benefit of order, efficiency, and driving. These plans featured superblocks, where enormous towers were surrounded by parks surrounded by multilane roadways. Completely lacking opportunities for pedestrian interaction or anything resembling the human scale, Le Corbusier's visions were never quite fully realized (though plenty of knockoff versions were).

Still, these efforts gave credence to the belief that driving and parking were the way forward for a city. They also set the stage for a generation of "towers in the park," where residential buildings were isolated from the street and retail—the kind of urban planning now almost universally derided. While today's best practices encourage human interaction, unique housing stock, abundant and distinctive retail, and walkability, back then the separation of residences, recreation, and car traffic was seen as truly cutting-edge.

As the resulting redesigned urban areas were neither full of nature and private space nor vibrant and walkable, car-oriented development only hastened the hollowing out of American cities and encouraged suburban development.

HERBERT HOOVER, THE inaugural secretary of the Department of Commerce, saw housing as a panacea for these uncertain times. Better quality, less expensive, more private housing was an easy thing to sell. Suburban development promoted calm, secluded living while cities grappled with crowding and immigration. It suggested a return to a nurturing, wholesome family life at a time when families were traumatized by the deaths of young men in the war. It reinforced women's role in the home just at the moment when women—who had entered the workforce in large numbers during the war—were being seen as unwelcome competition for returning soldiers and threatening to destabilize the reigning cultural order by agitating for equality and the right to vote.

While Hoover could hardly have guessed how successful housing would become as an industry and as a vehicle for wealth creation, he well understood that investing in real estate development and construction would generate a return for the country.

Hoover's insights into housing, both at Commerce and then a decade later as president, would set the stage for more aggressive federal policies to encourage homeownership in the wake of the Great Depression. For most of its preindustrial history, the federal government had taken a pretty laissez-faire approach to housing policy. That was changing, in a big way.

The first real attempt of the federal government to encourage single-family homeownership en masse was the 1918 "Own Your Own Home" campaign. Initially launched by a real estate advocacy group, the campaign was later supported by the Department of Labor and eventually housed at Hoover's Department of Commerce. Though the campaign stopped short of providing subsidies, it promoted the benefits of homeownership through pamphlets, posters, and lectures at universities; even children were given buttons to wear that said, "We own our own home."[1] Although the twenty-first-century YIMBY movement has yet to find a stronghold in national government, and isn't focused on homeownership, it feels as if YIMBYism inherited this campaign's tactics of pamphlets and buttons—and added social media and T-shirts—to further its mission of encouraging development.

Hoover's campaign did not materialize independently. Support for the Better Homes movement—a nationwide effort in the 1920s to encourage homeownership, home improvement, and interior decoration—had been building around the country. But Hoover was at the forefront as president of the board of directors of the Advisory Council of Better Homes in America, and as a supporter of frequent demonstrations and pamphlet campaigns espousing the importance of housing on both a personal and a patriotic level.[2] His 1922 essay "The Home as an Investment" laid out his philosophy from its first line: "One can always safely judge of the character of a nation by its homes."[3] He believed homes were bedrock for the country, that America could not be a great nation without housing for families that enabled them to achieve domestic comfort and financial stability.

Hoover considered adequate housing a moral imperative. As an orphan, he was sensitive to children's need for stability. And he wasn't alone in his concern for young people: books like *How the Other Half Lives* and incidents like the Triangle Shirtwaist Factory fire—where 146 garment factory workers, including girls as young as fourteen, perished—inspired widespread outrage over the appallingly dangerous living and working conditions for children in crowded cities. Reform movements in the early twentieth century sought to protect children who were vulnerable to unscrupulous bosses and parents. Hoover believed that by building new housing in the suburbs, he could help cities cope with overcrowding and a litany of related problems such as "a large increase in rents, a throw-back in human efficiency and that unrest which inevitably results from inhibition of the primal instinct in us all for home ownership."[4]

Suburban homeownership offered the promise of a better life for children. Homeownership, with its legal and financial entanglements, would prevent families from moving frequently. Its financial stability and upside would give families a hedge against squalor.

But the suburbs also went hand in hand with a set of social values that cities could no longer claim. As Kennesaw State University professor LeeAnn Lands writes in a paper discussing the links between homeownership and patriotism,

> By forging and delivering status rewards, federal and real estate interests encouraged new attention to homeownership a generation before tax write-offs, amortised mortgages, and federal mortgage insurance combined to make homeownership "affordable" to most Americans. Federal initiatives publicly associated the homeowner with thrift, character, moral fiber, and citizenship. Rhetoric imploring men to protect their families through homeownership was carefully deployed and reinforced. Homeowners were held up as patriots and family providers, the bulwark of the nation-state. National and local real estate interests and organizations followed, and then aligned renting and the renter with negative imagery, such as bolshevism and radicalism.[5]

While Hoover was promoting homes as the physical manifestation of family life, he also saw an emerging American industry.

Investing in the housing sector would produce a solid return to the country's economy in terms of jobs, tax revenue, and economic activity. Not only would this push bolster the post–World War I economy, but Hoover hoped it also would stave off the appeal of socialism and communism by enabling Americans to reap the fruits of capitalism. As secretary of the Department of Commerce, Hoover undertook a grand plan to standardize American housing elements, from bricks down to nails, to bring down the cost of housing and boost the productivity of home builders. He collaborated with the American Institute of Architects to create plans for model homes that could be built with these materials, hoping to cut housing costs by one-third.[6]

Hoover's quest to create efficiency and standards in housing also encouraged his interest in the role of zoning. The country's first zoning ordinance passed in 1908 in Los Angeles, and it primarily focused on separating residential and industrial zones. Cities like Baltimore and New Orleans followed with their own zoning codes in the 1920s—but there the intent was racial segregation. A 1917 Supreme Court decision, *Buchanan v. Warley*, would make race-based zoning ordinances illegal, but cities and suburbs found many other ways to enforce segregation. Ultimately, zoning gave legal cover to attempts to carve out neighborhoods and keep the areas where white and well-off people lived segregated.

In 1922, Hoover—still at the Department of Commerce—convened an advisory committee to issue the Standard State Zoning Enabling Act (SZEA), a fundamental piece of zoning legislation that endures a century later. The SZEA is important because of the way it gave cities and suburbs discretion to divide their municipalities into districts and enforce their own zoning through entities like zoning commissions. Notably, the SZEA calls out the purpose of zoning as the improvement of health and well-being. But this purpose has been disputed ever since, most recently in Richard Rothstein's chronicle of racism and segregation in American zoning, *The Color of Law*. He notes that Hoover's advisory committee on zoning, which espoused the importance of zoning for every municipality, "did not give the creation of racially homogenous neighborhoods as the reason why zoning should become such an important priority for cities, but the advisory committee was composed of outspoken segregationists whose speeches and writings demonstrated that race was one basis of their zoning advocacy."[7]

Zoning quickly came to prioritize single-family living over other housing types, as it was the bluntest tool to achieve class and racial segregation. By outlawing multifamily buildings, city governments could ensure that no tenements or rooming houses existed in certain neighborhoods. In 1926, the Supreme Court found single-family residential zoning as the "best and highest use" of land in Euclid, Ohio.[8] Rothstein notes that the decision "was a conspicuous exception of the Court's rejection of regulations that restricted what an owner could do with his property."[9] Typically, the law has favored property owners' rights to use their land or buildings for the purpose they see fit. Clearly this exception was based on something else: an effort to exclude certain types of people by excluding their residential needs or preferences.

That same year, the Supreme Court upheld the use of restrictive covenants. With covenants, property owners could list a set of requirements as part of the property deed. Owners could bluntly restrict future ownership to Caucasians, so that no black (or Jewish, or Asian, or otherwise marginalized) person could eventually own the property. So while a city's zoning ordinance could not be outright racist, per *Buchanan*, covenants often took on that role on a parcel-by-parcel basis. While the Supreme Court struck down racially restrictive covenants in 1948, and the Fair Housing Act outlawed them in 1968, their impact has endured decades later. Many metropolitan regions underwent their greatest growth periods in the first half of the twentieth century. Given the abundance of restrictive covenants that prohibited people of color and ethnic minorities from purchasing property in white neighborhoods at the time, cities today still grapple with the legacy of segregated neighborhoods. Nowadays, zoning and covenants regulate the minimum size for a house or a setback from a property line, but for much of the twentieth century they calibrated who, exactly, could live in a neighborhood.

Not only did single-family housing zones make the suburbs whiter and wealthier, they also separated residential areas from commercial activity and manufacturing. While zoning was originally conceived of as a way to address public health and safety concerns—from contagious diseases to toxic by-products of manufacturing activity—and encourage a connection with nature and sense of residential privacy, these ideals soon gave way to a heavily regulated development environment. Zoning also led to widespread environmental injustice, where buildings and institutions that wealthy people sought to avoid were located in low-income neighborhoods. It is no coincidence that plants, refineries, prisons, manufacturing facilities, and—later in the century—social services such as homeless shelters and drug rehabilitation centers were not built in wealthy, white neighborhoods. They were prohibited by the zoning in those neighborhoods.

From a real estate developer's perspective, zoning codes made standardized, suburban development easy and straightforward, allowing for a kind of never-before-seen expansion of housing in the country. In the 1920s, fast-paced construction transformed areas like Nassau County outside New York City and Berwyn just outside Chicago with hundreds of square miles of new housing.

Homeownership was integral to this new vision of housing. Many of these new suburban homes were not the McMansions we think of today, but rather small bungalows of one thousand square feet with a postage-stamp backyard. Still, according to Robert Bruegmann's account of twentieth-century suburban and exurban development, this upgrade to a house of one's own from a city rental represented "a real revolution in expectations" for many families.[10]

Owning a house in the suburbs equaled achievement. In his essay about investing in a home, Hoover writes, "There is no incentive to thrift like the ownership of property. The man who owns his own home has a happy sense of security. He will invest his hard earned savings to improve the house he owns. He will develop it and defend it. No man ever worked for, or fought for a boarding-house."[11]

Hoover—who, ironically, kept an apartment in the New York Waldorf Astoria hotel for thirty years after his presidency, and would die there in 1964—was right about the positive relationship between quality housing, financial upside, and security. But ultimately he had a too narrow view of the kind of housing—and the ownership structure—required to achieve these goals.

IN 1920, THE Census found that fewer than half—46 percent—of all Americans were homeowners. In cities, the figure was far lower. In New York City, for example, just 12 percent of residents were homeowners.[12] But in the 1920s, home mortgages in the country began to outnumber farm mortgages for the first time.[13] Whether it was Hoover's efforts, the Better Homes movement, or the new availability of single-family houses in the suburbs, homeownership rates were on the rise.

But by the end of the decade, the country was mired in the Great Depression. The fallout affected all areas of the economy, housing included. Between 1926 and 1932, the number of foreclosures tripled.[14] With no jobs to be had, few people could afford to buy houses, and many were bankrupted by the mortgages on their properties. The federal government had to act to pull Americans—and the economy—out of the slump.

During the Great Depression, the federal government sought to stabilize housing markets and stoke the housing and construction industries through a series of policies. As a result, the Depression served as a major catalyst for new housing policies and programs that heavily ramped up the federal government's involvement in and subsidies toward housing. Most of the new programs were aimed at boosting homeownership and preventing foreclosures. Many of them would become pillars of the housing industry for decades to come.

In 1932, the Federal Home Loan Bank Act attempted to fix the problems created by inadequate supply of credit by creating a network of twelve commercial banks that could borrow funds from the treasury and, in turn, loan that money to small, local banks where mortgages originated.

The next year, the Home Owners Loan Act was passed, establishing the Home Owners' Loan Corporation (HOLC), an entity that enabled millions of American homeowners to refinance their mortgages and avoid foreclosure. HOLC existed for just four years, but it left a lasting legacy beyond the homeowners it helped: its system of color-coded maps, which attempted to assess the risk of lending in neighborhoods based on demographics. Predominantly white neighborhoods were considered low-risk for lending and coded white; predominantly minority neighborhoods were considered risky, coded red. These racist maps were used by banks and government entities for decades after HOLC's dissolution; the term "redlining" originates from the practice of financing homes only outside the red zones on HOLC maps.

In 1934, the National Housing Act established the Federal Housing Administration (FHA). To this day, the FHA sets standards for underwriting mortgages. Though its goal was and remains ensuring stability in the mortgage market, its tools for understanding neighborhood stability have never been nuanced, and in the past were overtly racist. In the 1930s, the risk of potential default for any given mortgage was seen as higher if that neighborhood was a racially integrated one. Majority-minority neighborhoods were considered too risky to invest in—not only during the Great Depression, but for decades afterward. Even in 2020, the FHA will not underwrite mortgages for condominiums where the majority of units are rented rather than owned.

Fannie Mae and Freddie Mac, known today for their role in the 2008 financial crisis, were first created in 1938 to help homeowners get a mortgage and in return help small local banks increase their liquidity. Whereas before banks could only lend to a few low-risk home buyers able to put up a substantial down payment, these banks now could lend to a wider set of borrowers, enable them to get a mortgage with as little as 3 percent down, and then sell those mortgages to Fannie and

Freddie. Critical to the mortgage market, Fannie and Freddie would guarantee small banks' loans, so even if the borrower foreclosed, the bank where the mortgage originated was no longer at risk. Finally, by offering standard fixed-rate mortgages for longer terms (thirty years instead of five or seven) with less money down, the government made it possible for the first time ever for many families to afford to own a home.

These programs and pieces of legislation exclusively focused on homeownership—specifically, homeownership that was safe enough to write a loan against: a single-family home in an all-white neighborhood. Remarkably, the government had essentially no plans to support people of color or renters, other than to create public housing.

THE POLICIES ENACTED in the 1930s created the backbone of American housing policy. They established the framework for financing, construction, and regulation for the next century. Ingrained in the policy was an approach to standardizing housing through materials, mortgages, and even consumers. In the 1930s, '40s, and '50s, the United States was a relatively homogeneous country dominated by white, middle-class, heterosexual norms and family-oriented housing—and federal housing policies worked to keep it that way.

Because the policies created were not inclusive of nonwhite communities, disparities between whites and people of color would only grow. Homeowners would have an advantage that would extend across generations, while renters would only be further stigmatized and deprived of financial upside.

The 1930s also witnessed the first widespread creation of public housing in America. The Housing Act of 1937 allowed for federal subsidies for public housing authorities. The act has been amended multiple times since—enabling some of the country's most important housing legislation, from the funding of slum clearance in 1949 to the creation of Section 8 housing vouchers in 1974. Public housing's initial goal was to house people temporarily, as millions of Americans were newly destitute due to the Depression. These "worthy poor" were living not only in cities, but also in rural areas. As a result of both the location and the sympathy extended to those being housed, early public housing bore little resemblance to the projects that we now associate with it. Of the ninety-nine communities built as part of the New Deal, forty were located in rural or suburban communities.[15] Moreover, the federal Farm Security Administration paid architects to design and build cooperative migrant camps for fifteen thousand families, complete with Israeli kibbutz–inspired community centers and day cares.[16]

Given the state of much contemporary public housing, it is hard to believe the level of craftsmanship in the public housing of the 1930s. During the Depression, public housing built by the Public Works Administration with involvement of the Works Projects Administration featured artfully sculpted friezes, and "even the smallest projects featured copper roofs, elaborate brickwork and canopies over every door."[17] Whereas the public housing of the 1930s and '40s had a human scale and local character—and was seen as a temporary support system for people who'd been made destitute by the Depression—by the 1950s its style and purpose had changed. At that point, the country was juggling the costs of the Korean War and no longer sought to invest heavily in public housing.

Quality housing for the poor also didn't align with the national homeownership ethos of thrift and hard work for the reward of private property. Here we see the beginnings of a debate over how to build and sustain publicly funded, affordable housing in the United States. Whereas European countries would invest heavily in social housing as a way to recover from World War II—and some cities, like Vienna and Copenhagen, would create such high-quality public housing that it has become ingrained in the culture and livability of those cities—policymakers in the United States were mixed in their feelings about how much to subsidize housing.

American emphasis on the "virtue" of homeownership—rooted in both self-sufficiency and sacrifice—deeply conflicted with providing housing below market cost. Public housing at this time was considered so well-built that residential market-rate developers and realtors actually feared it would discourage homeownership.[18] The housing industry, having been built up and supported by the government, was now powerful enough to push back on housing policy. As a result, public housing had to look and feel different enough that it could be easily distinguished from privately owned housing. Communities often reserved residential density for public housing, thereby adding stigma to any multifamily housing, no matter if it was aimed at market-rate owners or renters.

While the government was investing in public housing, another plank of housing policy became the elimination of substandard private homes in cities through a massive slum clearance program. In 1949, the Housing and Slum Clearance Act authorized $1.5 billion in federal funds to raze whole neighborhoods where housing was deemed substandard and build 810,000 units in their place.[19] The construction industry had a say in how slum clearance rolled out, requiring the "equivalent elimination" of slum housing for each new unit of housing created. By managing the number of available housing units, builders could ensure housing would remain scarce enough to warrant a high price point.

By 1966, some four hundred thousand housing units had been cleared and three hundred thousand households (more than half of which were people of color) forcibly relocated. Even though the new, dense housing that replaced the relatively low-rise tenements and brownstones was not public housing, the two were conflated. Density was equated with urban poverty, and urban poverty with people of color. Not only would people become segregated by race and class, but so would the structures they lived in. In addition to decimating people's homes and the historic character of many cities with slum clearance, the government supported the construction of additional infrastructure and highways to enable access to the suburbs, further deepening the appeal of these neighborhoods for those who could afford them.

Cheap, segregated, and isolated housing created a vicious downward cycle that was hard for urban residents—largely people of color—to escape. Despite public concern over how to help the poor, programs that intentionally sought to extend the benefits of homeownership to excluded minorities were not implemented for decades.

FOLLOWING WORLD WAR II, the United States doubled down on developing the suburbs. The social conformity that would consume the country was just one outgrowth of confidence in the American lifestyle. While the process of suburbanization and sprawl had begun in the previous century, it hit its stride with the creation of the federal highway system and new interventions to support single-family homeownership.

In the postwar period, the government deployed a series of changes to the federal income-tax system that made homeownership even more desirable, including allowing homeowners to deduct local property taxes and rental income from their adjusted gross income. When this was combined with the long-standing ability to deduct mortgage interest, Americans were essentially penalized for not owning a home. In addition, Congress authorized the Servicemen's Readjustment Act of 1944, better known as the GI Bill. Among the bill's many benefits conveyed to veterans was a provision allowing them to secure a mortgage without a down payment and with a below-market interest rate. Due to these interventions, the percentage of owner-occupied households increased from 44 to 62 percent between 1940 and 1960.[20]

The easy access to mortgages and home building combined with population growth (due in part to the notorious baby boom) and a decrease in average household size (due to more elderly people living alone) to create an explosion of sprawl. The United States added fifty million people in the two decades after World War II, reaching a population of two hundred million. In the sunny cities of the south and west, population growth was even more explosive. Los Angeles doubled from four to eight million people, while San Jose quintupled its urbanized area.[21]

Additionally, new prefabrication techniques and advances in manufacturing made residential construction easier, faster, and cheaper. The success of these suburban culs-de-sac was largely contingent on uniformity. Perhaps the best-known example of the new suburban communities was Levittown, Long Island—which was one of seven similar suburban developments created by William Levitt. Levitt became the country's largest developer in the postwar era, capable of producing a product and selling it at a speed unlike anything the country has seen since: When he first offered his houses for sale in 1949, he went into contract on some 1,400 homes on the first day. By 1950, his factory was able to produce a four-room house every sixteen minutes.

Though the demand for this kind of housing would suggest that it handily satisfied the needs of families, not everyone was convinced by its merits. A backlash against the suburbs came soon enough, whether from urbanist writers like Jane Jacobs and Lewis Mumford or from housewives living in suburbia themselves. In 1956, the federal government convened a Women's Congress on Housing that brought dozens of housewives to Washington to discuss their social and economic concerns with suburban lifestyles. The Rockwellian good life wasn't always what it seemed, and a slew of art, film, and literature—like Sloan Wilson's *The Man in the Gray Flannel Suit* (1955) and Richard Yates's *Revolutionary Road* (1961)—portrayed the suburbs as soulless, isolating places where the ideals of a comfortable family life for children had subsumed the needs of adults. The suburbs also reinforced a patriarchal vision of power, where men commuted to the city and earned the family's money while women tended to the children and household upkeep at home.

In the 1960s, books like Jacobs's *The Death and Life of Great American Cities* sang the praises of free-form urban life, but with a more research-based urban-planning approach. The social isolation and lack of diverse amenities typical of the suburbs (and in many modern urban developments) were the natural effects of their architecture, planning, and zoning, and the way in which they denied natural human tendencies to build dense, diverse communities. This discourse, along with major federal investment in housing, resulted in a big shift in urban development trends. By the mid-1960s there were more multifamily homes being built in many metropolitan areas than single-family ones.[22]

DESPITE EFFORTS TO improve urban life, the disparities between urban and suburban, rented and owned, black and white, had only grown by the late 1960s. The Kerner Commission, convened by President Lyndon Johnson to look at the causes of social unrest in the country, noted that "our Nation is moving toward two societies, one black, one white—separate and unequal."[23] Black Americans lagged behind white Americans in educational attainment, employment, homeownership, and other key indicators of economic mobility.

To address the growing inequality in the country, Johnson implemented a series of social justice policies collectively called the Great Society. Perhaps best known for its War on Poverty, the Great Society agenda ranged from the creation of Medicare to the establishment of the Department of Housing and Urban Development (HUD). HUD was tasked with creating a tremendous amount of affordable housing. Prior to the Great Society, the creation of affordable housing in the United States had peaked at seventy-one thousand units in 1954; during the Great Society, HUD helped produce nearly five hundred thousand units annually during a four-year growth period.[24]

In addition to HUD's efforts to increase the supply of affordable housing, Congress passed legislation aimed at undoing some of the damage done by redlining. The Fair Housing Act of 1968, part of a broader package of civil rights legislation, attempted to ensure that realtors did not use race as a reason for showing—or not showing—certain neighborhoods to certain clients. But despite making it illegal to practice housing discrimination, the law was rarely effectual in punishing bad actors, and HUD, the lead authority tasked with dealing with complaints, has never had the capacity to manage the full extent of reports of discrimination.

Increased production of affordable housing and progressive, anti-racist legislation should have been big wins for housing advocates. Yet in the 1970s, the United States saw stagnating wages, consistent increases in taxes, and continued urban decline, despite heavy investments in public housing. Ronald Reagan's 1980 presidential campaign became a referendum on government involvement in solving social challenges. Reagan's classic line that "government isn't the solution, it's the problem" offered a paradigm shift that appealed to many voters. He won the election with a nine-point lead in the popular vote and a true landslide electoral college victory. Much of the country felt ready for a reset, with Reagan promising a smaller government and lower taxes.

To be sure, while the roots of public housing's failure, of cities' decline, and of middle-class angst were complex, the government had not proven itself to be a good steward of the housing it had, nor was it clear about its plan to support subsidized housing. An infamous example was the Pruitt-Igoe housing project in Saint Louis. The thirty-three eleven-story buildings had been built to replace the DeSoto-Carr slums, where approximately two-thirds of the five thousand dwellings had no toilets. Despite being designed by renowned architect Minoru Yamasaki, the Pruitt-Igoe complex began facing setbacks long before construction even began. In the years after it opened, it rapidly descended into squalor due to a combination of a lack of services, ghettoization of the poor, and racism. Within a decade, Pruitt-Igoe was unlivable, and residents who could afford to live elsewhere had left. In the 1970s, it would be evacuated and finally demolished live on television. To this day, Saint Louis has never rebuilt on the site.

At the same time, cities were continuing to hemorrhage residents to the suburbs, not only due to white flight but also because of the deindustrialization of the economy. As metropolitan areas underwent a shift from manufacturing and related industries to white-collar professional services, the location and type of jobs available also changed. Saint Louis, whose population peaked in 1950 with 856,796 people, had lost four hundred thousand residents by 1980. In the same time period, Detroit lost six hundred thousand people (nearly one-third of its population), and Philadelphia lost four hundred thousand (nearly one-quarter of its population).

Not every US city experienced such devastating declines. Boston saw only mild population decreases during this period, and San Francisco essentially kept a flat population during the 1970s and '80s. But even to these cities, it would have seemed unthinkable that there would come a day when so many people—and high-income individuals in particular—wanted to live there that the housing supply wouldn't be able to keep up with demand.

In the 1980s, as cities dealt with population declines and low tax revenues, many city governments began to ask how neighborhoods could be revived. Whereas urban policy strategies today are more likely focused on jobs, throughout the 1980s and '90s mayors focused on quality-of-life issues. As core cities competed with their wealthier suburbs, many sought to promote how upscale their business and cultural districts could be. Small projects (like renaming Broad Street in Philadelphia as Avenue of the Arts) and major ones (like the decade-long replacement of a six-lane elevated highway known as the Big Dig in Boston) sought to recast cities as welcoming of tourists and investment. Transient housing, single room occupancies (SROs), and apartment hotels—all of which helped lower-income people live close to the city's core—did not fit within this new urban paradigm and came under attack. By the end of the century, these types of housing were largely outlawed in most major cities.

At the same time, long-standing demographic patterns began to shift as baby boomers entered their thirties. Multigenerational housing hit its lowest point in American history and average household size began a steep decline. Women began entering the workforce at higher rates than ever, further delaying the age of first marriage and first child. Baby boomers were having fewer children than their parents, and deciding against having children became less stigmatized. Rates of living alone began to rise. Additionally, the Reagan administration's changes to government aid policy created new barriers, which kept families from living together if their combined household income exceeded the poverty level and other thresholds for accessing aid.

In combination with these timely developments, city-sponsored gentrification worked. The 1980s and '90s witnessed massive appreciation in real estate values in major cities' prime neighborhoods. Additionally, many municipalities added an array of regulations intended to elevate the quality of new developments in an attempt to maintain property values. Minimum lot- and house-size requirements became commonplace, as did restrictions on the kind and number of materials that could be used on the exterior. Not surprisingly, the permitting and approvals process for building housing became more onerous and time-consuming. Housing and planning scholar John Landis noted in a 2000 study on California development, "Based on a diverse sample of 24 single-family subdivisions and 22 multifamily developments entitled between 1995 and 1998, the average single-family development project involved 3.3 separate development reviews and was approved in just under a year." Multifamily projects were approved in a slightly quicker fashion but still felt the burden. Landis concludes that the difficulty of building housing and aligning a product to local authorities' requests often meant that only large-scale, well-capitalized home builders had the capacity to "cope with the process."[25]

Americans living and owning in the best areas absorbed the idea that housing wasn't just about home, privacy, or neighborhoods anymore; it was an investment. Housing outperformed the stock market and just about any other asset. In the coming decades, buyers and investors would push housing investment as far as the market would allow.

In cities, a growing cohort of people valued the walkability, multipurpose buildings, and vibrancy of urban places. Many homeowners were also excited about appreciating real estate values there. In Manhattan, for example, housing prices went up on average by 185 percent between 1996 and 2006.[26] As globalization started to hit its stride, cities like New York attracted foreign buyers looking to cash in on a rising market. For the first time in a century, cities grew at a faster pace than suburbs.

But the exurbs—those less-dense areas farther from the metropolitan core than the regular suburbs—grew faster still (by 31 percent in the 1990s alone) and were home to more than 60 percent of new manufacturing jobs.[27] The high cost of housing, deliberate gentrification, and restrictive zoning combined to make it difficult to build more housing for the middle class in cities through the end of the 1990s and early 2000s. As a result, to find mid-priced housing, people moved farther and farther from the city core.

By the early 2000s, anyone who had the funds on hand to participate in the housing market could hardly afford to be left out of it—the opportunity cost of sitting on the sidelines while prices rose every week was simply too high. While the 1990s and early 2000s saw a boom in construction and increasing housing prices, these were extensions of trends long established over the past fifty years. It felt as though they could continue forever—and in fact it seemed like the situation was accelerating. It was this kind of thinking that led people to bring checkbooks to open houses, offering down payments on the spot. No wonder more than 69 percent of Americans were homeowners at the peak of the housing market in 2006.[28]

Banks offered loans that took advantage of the buyer's predicament, including "no doc" mortgages that allowed buyers to skip the income-vetting process for a mortgage and qualify for loans they often couldn't afford. Unlike the mortgages with more stringent requirements in the past, these so-called subprime loans were offered to almost anyone who asked for one. Banks accounted for the higher risk of foreclosure by charging a higher rate of interest, leading to monthly costs far above what many borrowers could afford. These mortgages might have worked in the sunny housing atmosphere of the early 2000s. But they did not take into account what would happen to these buyers—and to the country and to the idea of homeownership—if there was a major recession or housing downturn.

CHAPTER THREE

MISMATCHED HOUSING AND DEMOGRAPHICS

WHILE THE GREAT RECESSION would not officially begin until December 2007, housing prices started to decline in the beginning of 2006, going into free fall by the end of the year. Though demand had increased, inventory far exceeded it. Additionally, the housing industry—like most other businesses at the time—had globalized and consolidated to access new sources of funding and reap greater profits. Whereas small home builders got their financing by convincing a bank there was a market and little risk in building new homes, large home builders' financing from global capital markets encouraged more risk in search of more reward. With their economies of scale and cushioned balance sheet, these companies could withstand failure.

The American economy for the past decade had been driven in no small part by the buying and selling of homes. A study by the Center for Economic and Policy Research noted that

67

"for the two decades prior to the start of the run-up in house prices in the late 1990s, residential construction averaged less than 4.5 percent of GDP. At its peak in the fourth quarter of 2005, residential construction was almost 6.8 percent of GDP. A slow-down in the housing sector would have far-reaching effects."[1] Not only would a decline in the housing market cause the construction industry to grind to a halt, but it would affect real estate brokerage, furniture production, and everything else, down to the ads in interior decoration magazines. Most immediately, the mortgage industry had either miscalculated (or feigned confidence in) how many subprime borrowers would pay their mortgages. Once the prices of homes had declined so much that the cost of the loans outweighed the worth of a home, more homeowners would walk away from their mortgages.

Between 2007 and 2012, more than 12.5 million homes went into foreclosure.[2] It was a crisis for which the closest comparison, in terms of the scale of personal misfortune, was the Great Depression. Given that the federal government responded to the Great Depression's foreclosure crisis with a series of programs that incentivized and supported homeownership, one might have expected a similar set of policies this time around. Certainly the Great Recession merited such a response because of the financial disaster wrought on households. But government priorities had changed in the preceding decades.

The Great Recession marked a true turning point in federal housing policy. While most of the federal response to the housing downturn focused on preventing foreclosure by refinancing loans and creating new payment plans, the rhetoric of government intervention in housing had changed. Georgia State University professor Dan Immergluck remarks in a paper about responses to the foreclosure crisis that these programs were "tentative, incremental and marginal."[3] These efforts were no match for the reality of the mortgage-servicing industry, which isn't built to prevent foreclosure—in fact, it's incentivized to make money off it.

Rather than encourage individual homeownership as a path back to financial stability, the Barack Obama administration's primary response was neighborhood focused. The government established the Neighborhood Stabilization Program (NSP) to give grants to state and local authorities to purchase foreclosed properties, in order to secure neighborhoods from the ravages of the foreclosure crisis. By putting the properties in government hands, municipalities could ensure they were redeveloped and resold to low- and moderate-income households. While there were some NSP programs that gave down-payment assistance to homeowners for purchasing foreclosed properties as well, they accounted for just 6 percent of overall NSP spending. By contrast, 66 percent was spent on local entities' acquisition and rehabilitation of foreclosed properties.[4]

Still, in many communities, NSP-led efforts to strategically purchase properties were thwarted by investors, who could purchase property more quickly in the private market. As the NSP focused on redevelopment and occupancy, private equity companies purchased tens of thousands of foreclosed properties at a fraction of their prerecession cost. In a new twist, these houses weren't resold at higher prices when the market recovered. Instead, they were turned into rentals. Invitation Homes, originally financed through multinational private-equity firm Blackstone, bought up thousands of homes and now markets itself as a purveyor of updated homes with professional property management in sixteen markets across the country.[5] A number of real estate investment trusts essentially ran the same business. Heavy investment in a new asset class of rentals not only changed the inventory in many communities, but also set the stage for venture-capital-financed co-living. Ten years after the recession, investors would be primed to invest in co-living because they'd experienced the upside of investing in mass-market rentals.

Not only was the government unable to rescue a sufficient number of homeowners, but it was outmaneuvered by the private sector, which could move more nimbly and with greater profit motive. The government also had to reckon with the downside of its long-held homeownership strategy: How could the state continue to promote homeownership as a path to stability and wealth creation when it had equal potential to wreck people's finances? One of the highlights of Congress's response was the Dodd-Frank Wall Street Reform and Consumer Protection Act, enacted in 2010, which limited banks' investment in risky lending practices when also lending to homeowners.

A return to normal was no longer possible. Parts of the country were overbuilt and had high vacancy rates. Between the first quarter of 2006 and the third quarter of 2012, the American housing market lost $7 trillion in home equity, and a total of 22 percent of homeowners were saddled with "underwater" mortgages.[6] Between 2006 and 2014, ten million Americans lost their homes in foreclosures—an astounding figure that accounts for about one in twelve households.[7] The homeownership rate sank from a peak of 69.2 percent in 2004 to a bottom of 62.9 in 2016, before leveling off at about 64 percent. That 5 percent or so drop represents a net loss of nearly four million homeowners in the recession.

The effects of the Great Recession varied greatly based on region, ethnic group, and price range. For example, Las Vegas real estate experienced a 59 percent drop in home values, whereas Denver saw declines of just 10 percent. Minorities bore the brunt of the recession. The Pew Research Center reported that from 2005 to 2009 Hispanic households saw median wealth decline by 66 percent and black households by 53 percent, while white households only witnessed a loss of 16 percent. Finally, lower-priced homes saw the greatest upward price swings and the deepest declines, while the wealthiest homeowners faced less of a loss proportionally and recovered more quickly.

With homeownership rates remaining down 5 percent, it's evident that only some of the people who suffered the pain of the downturn were able to experience the gain when prices bounced back. The mortgage industry underwent a number of reforms that made lending criteria tighter, requiring higher credit scores, more money down, and more information at the time of issuing a loan. All of this meant that the difference between homeowners and renters a decade after the recession was even vaster: homeowners were whiter and wealthier, with higher credit scores.

While the average property suffered a 33 percent decline, it would rebound by 50 percent between the market's bottom and 2018.[8] Because the housing downturn was accompanied by a great rise in unemployment, there were fewer individuals who could take advantage of newly low real estate prices. Housing prices would far exceed prerecession figures in some markets, such as San Francisco, Seattle, Washington, DC, and New York. In those cities, there was a steady influx of wealthy, educated buyers whose salaries enabled higher price points—not only in housing, but in everything from food to clothing to basic services. Despite seeing population increases and gentrification of goods and services, there was comparatively little housing construction in these cities. Supply was constricted by a tight and lengthy regulatory process for building new housing, and new construction was sidelined by the increase in rental properties.

Homeownership in America faced some existential questions: How could people enter into a mortgage agreement again when they had lost their jobs in the Great Recession and had a high risk of defaulting on the loan? Why promote a homeownership-focused urban policy when it had so poorly served people of color? In a world of globalized capital and lending, how should the government intervene?

WHILE MARKET AND government activities set the stage for a dramatically different future of housing, demographic conditions ensured it would be different following the recession. The recession and its aftermath occurred at the time when millennials, the country's largest demographic group ever, were predominantly in their twenties and thirties. For other demographic groups, this life phase would have been a time of getting married, having kids, and buying houses. The recession not only wiped out wealth that might have been used to buy new homes, but it also lowered confidence in housing as an investment that would always appreciate. Born in the 1980s and '90s, millennials grew up during the digital revolution and in an environment of constant change. Unlike members of past generations, who might have expected their lives to resemble that of their parents but better, millennials, who have significantly more student debt and lower net worths than previous generations, had no such illusions.[9]

Many trends that had been brewing in American culture reached fruition in the millennial generation. Whereas freelancing and holding multiple jobs had been growing in popularity, its prevalence increased as millennials reached their twenties. The recession had also reshaped the economy, so that more millennials were working multiple jobs, piecing together part-time work, or preferring not to take on the demands of a full-time job.

Likewise, millennials own fewer cars and homes than previous generations did at their age. There is research and anecdotal evidence to suggest that millennials prefer not to own things and favor experiences over the freighted responsibility of ownership.[10] Car ownership—previously considered a rite of passage—has dropped in popularity as young people have turned to Uber, scooters, and bike shares. The popularity of companies such as Rent the Runway and Airbnb point to an ease with renting everything from clothes to cars to houses.

Millennials also tend to have less sex, have fewer close friends, and feel lonely more often than other demographics.[11] As a result, this has made the model of pairing off and buying a home together less likely. (Marriage increases the chances of homeownership by 18 percent.)[12] It has also opened the door to increased co-living, and, as many millennials moved back home during the Great Recession, multigenerational housing.

Underlying many of these preferences is an economic reality. Contrary to the research that says millennials are blazing new lifestyles that better represent their true desires, there is also evidence that suggests they would prefer to own but can't afford to. Whether personal preference or increased debt combined with decreased earning potential is driving low millennial homeownership rates—just 39 percent of white millennials and 14.5 percent of black millennials—the resulting decrease in lifetime home purchases and wealth creation remains the same.[13]

BY THE 2010S, as people grew frustrated with the lack of housing that was affordable even by middle-class standards, politicians and housing advocacy groups sought new ways to preserve affordability in cities. Some cities, like Seattle, sought to create a "head tax" on companies such as Amazon and Microsoft. The legislation that the Seattle City Council proposed, and later killed, would have required major companies to pay $200 per employee into a housing trust fund. Yet the tens of millions of dollars that tax would have generated would have produced fewer than two thousand housing units—a pitiful number given that nearly half of all Seattle residents are "housing burdened," or paying more than 30 percent of their income on housing.[14] Other cities, such as Boston, relied on inclusionary zoning, requiring that all developments either pay into the affordable housing trust fund or build affordable housing on-site. But research has shown that inclusionary zoning laws not only result in very small numbers of affordable units per year (only a few hundred in cities like Boston and Washington, DC), they also cause the market-rate portion of a development to be more expensive.[15]

Other regions have opted for a new kind of strategy— neither carrot nor stick. They saw getting rid of existing barriers as the best way to encourage more production of housing at lower cost, and took aim at their own restrictive single-family zoning regulations. In California, over the course of a decade, advocates pushed for reform of accessory dwelling unit laws. Prior to reform, each accessory dwelling unit needed its own parking and had onerous setback laws and stringent size requirements. As a result, only a few hundred ADUs were built in a state with some 750,000 detached single-family homes. Following ADU reform, the permit rate went up tenfold.[16]

Meanwhile, cities grappling with the effects of unaffordable housing began to look at the inherent problems with the single-family home. Conversations started that challenged long-standing assumptions about what developers and constituents wanted. Namely, in desirable cities it was hard to imagine how to get the number of homes necessary to accommodate a growing population while so much land was set aside for single-family housing.

In 2018 in Minneapolis, a thirty-seven-year-old named Jacob Frey was elected mayor on a platform that addressed affordable housing. Coupled with a diverse and progressive city council, the mayor was able to pass a bill to rezone the entire city so that anything up to a triplex could be built. Minneapolis saw this as an opportunity to address its racial segregation, and it inspired other states like Oregon and Washington to do the same.

Working in tandem with progressive governments to enact these zoning changes was an unusual coalition of housing advocates. It wasn't just affordable housing groups, but also YIMBY groups, developers, and constituent groups like AARP.[17] As they collectively began to explore the root causes of a lack of housing at all price points, many came back to single-family housing and its flaws. If a piece of land could be zoned for one single-family home or a four-story building, which one would provide more housing? And which one was going to be cheaper per unit? And which one was going to be more environmentally sustainable? It became harder and harder for anyone—aside from NIMBYs (that is, "not in my backyard") hoping to preserve their property values—to avoid the logic in building more dense housing.

The result wasn't just a few legislative wins here and there. It was nothing less than a nationwide social movement challenging the status quo in housing.

THEY SAY EVERYTHING old is new again, but for housing that may actually be true. Zoning reform, new housing start-ups, and changing lifestyles have paved the way for a return to the housing types described in Chapter One, but with a modern twist. Like in the 1800s, people are transient again, moving to cities without connections and living in temporary housing before settling somewhere. The household nowadays is also looking less like a nuclear family and more improvised. "Family" can mean kids from numerous marriages, in-house relatives, and grandfamilies, where grandparents are primary caretakers. At the same time, more people are living alone.

Homeowners themselves have changed. While limited liability companies (LLCs) didn't exist before the 1970s, they now represent a major segment of home buyers. Foreign buyers owned about 183,000 properties valued at $77.9 billion during a period from April 2018 to March 2019, down from 266,800 properties and $121 billion the previous year, before the Donald Trump administration's tariffs on China and other nationalist policies.[18]

It's clear the housing policy landscape of the twenty-first century will be different than the twentieth-century status quo. The brave new future of housing must involve a return to something that values diversity, flexibility, and community, while responding to modern preferences and trends.

PART TWO

NEW WAYS OF LIVING

CHAPTER FOUR

LIVING BETTER, TOGETHER

COMING HOME FROM SCHOOL as a child, Gillian Morris was never sure whom she might find. Her family's home in the 1990s suburbs of New York had an open-door policy toward guests. There was always a visiting musician, a family friend whose house was being renovated and needed to stay for a few months, a distant cousin in town for the week. Evenings were filled with characters from around the world who exposed her to new ideas and new places through their conversations around the dinner table. "We had a wonderful, dynamic mix of people," Morris recalls. "So that made me assume this was the way it was for most people." As she grew older, she came to realize that her family was an outlier.

Given her upbringing, it may not be surprising that Morris went on to launch a travel app, Hitlist, that allows people to search for airfares like "JFK to anywhere" and find cheap flights across the globe. By Morris's midtwenties, she was splitting time between New York, San Francisco, and the road, but she wanted a home base. Her definition of "home" reflected her roots. Home meant a sense of community and interesting people coming and going. Thinking back to her childhood, she said, "I loved that openness of sharing space with other people, but I wasn't going to get it from a regular apartment."

So Morris, Melissa Kwan (another app entrepreneur), and Michael Gruen (another tech worker) started a "commune" in a twenty-two-foot-wide Manhattan town house. "Commune" might carry a whiff of patchouli, but this is a decidedly different shared space. Morris and Kwan's Gramercy House does triple duty: a home for the two of them, rooms for an additional three people, and a salon for entertaining. It took a while to find a landlord who was comfortable with the concept (their landlord still bugs them about "foot traffic"), but for the past four years the house's 1,500 square feet of entertaining space have hosted everything from meditation sessions to political fundraisers. With a dining table that seats sixteen and a parlor boasting ample seating, a faux-vintage oriental rug, and midcentury coffee table, the modest but chic space is ready to host a party any night of the week.

Gramercy House was a forerunner of co-living and is a small-scale application of what has become a full-blown asset class, garnering hundreds of millions in investment around the country. While the definition and implementation of co-living vary from places as small as Gramercy House to buildings housing hundreds of people, there are some key commonalities and ways to distinguish co-living from an apartment shared among friends or a condo building with amenities.

Co-living prioritizes the shared spaces of the house or building, both in terms of how much square footage the shared space is afforded and how it is programmed. While hosting a concert or yoga classes would be kind of weird in a regular apartment, public programming is expected in a co-living space. Whereas most living situations offer plain shelter, co-living is intentionally focused on community building.

Historically, the shared aspect of living with strangers was a drawback. In the boardinghouses and SROs of yore, residents got a room of their own at a lower cost in exchange for sharing a bathroom or kitchen. But the new co-living model emphasizes communality as a selling point. Whereas the default expectation in a normal apartment building is to keep to oneself, in co-living arrangements there's an open invitation to connect with people in common spaces. Since social interaction may not happen organically, operators put on programming—ranging from communal dinners to gym classes to off-site trips—to bring residents together and break the ice.

The co-living business model in many ways emulates the success of co-working in the 2010s. Co-working upended the traditional office rental landscape, which favored established businesses with long-term leases and oversize footprints. Recognizing the market for office space for small businesses and solo entrepreneurs, co-working offered not only greater flexibility but a host of other benefits like networking, all-inclusive rents, free coffee, and attention to design. Major co-living operators like Common, WeLive, Ollie, and X Social Communities now offer many of the same benefits, swapping "community" for "networking." Like co-working, co-living offers people the opportunity to rent square footage in a location that they might not be able to afford if they had to take on a lease entirely on their own.

ON A SUMMER night in 2018, I join Morris and some other co-living enthusiasts in Gramercy House's parlor. Barefoot, in keeping with the house rules, we sip wine and mango-avocado smoothies and feast on homemade pizzettas, cherries, and halvah before diving into the night's subject: the advantages and challenges of co-living. From the dozen or so attendees, we hear about an array of co-living situations: There's Jason from the Archive in San Francisco, a space housing sixteen people in tech and "tech adjacent" fields. There's Eric from the Embassy Network, an international organization of "place-based communities experimenting with new forms of governance and solidarity." There's a woman from a "sex-positive" three-story commune called Hacienda in the Brooklyn neighborhood of Bedford-Stuyvesant. Also visiting from Brooklyn is the founder of a co-living space called Lightning Society in Bushwick—a neighborhood with plenty of new co-living houses popping up each year.

What has driven these people and the others in the room to become ambassadors of and entrepreneurs in co-living? It's clear co-living has helped this crowd live their lives to the fullest, without the restrictions that standardized housing might put on them. There's Ethan, who works as a programmer and only needs a laptop and Wi-Fi to work. Because he doesn't need to live in one place or city, he's gravitated toward a nomadic lifestyle. He talks about how he spent the last month bopping around Europe, staying at spaces like Outsite in Lisbon, a co-living and co-working community for professionals. Outsite offers a global membership for remote workers, allowing them to explore working and living at locations ranging from New York City to Tulum, Mexico, to Santiago, Chile. At Outsite, he not only met new people but reconnected with friends and acquaintances in a beautiful locale.

Morris chimes in about the global digital nomad community. During her recent two-week stint in Berlin, she encoun-
tered friends from several San Francisco communes. A female
entrepreneur who runs a lifestyle company out of Los Angeles
and is staying at the Gramercy House during her time in New
York explains that her loyalty to co-living comes from connections and conversations like this one. Where else could she find
a dozen nomadic people whose values so clearly align with hers?

While co-living might seem like a subculture, it is quickly
turning into a widespread phenomenon and real estate asset
class. Investors are pouring money into developments with
hundreds of units. In contrast, these pioneers at Gramercy
House look more like mom-and-pop co-living operators.

The conversation turns to the nitty-gritty of running co-
living communities: How do you maintain a sense of belonging
and friendship with a close community of ten or more people? What software do you use to manage shared budgeting
decisions? Should you get rid of living rooms in favor of bigger kitchens and dining rooms? "It's been scientifically proven,
through studies where they put trackers on people, that no one
uses living rooms," says David, a writer for Co-Liv Lab, a networking organization for people in the business of co-living.
It's true, at least according to the most famous study on the
subject, by UCLA researchers who tracked thirty-two dual-
earner couples and found that formal dining and living spaces
(as well as yards) were underused.[1]

The challenges of co-living don't sound so bad to me, although those present have a few negative stories to share. In
small communes like Gramercy House, the experience of one
"guy who didn't work out" meant a few frustrating months and

lessons learned about better screening of long-term roommates. And Lisa, who's living in a co-living/working space in Bed-Stuy, is getting pushed out by a landlord who wants to sell the building. But rather than give up on co-living, she's here tonight to learn more about starting her own space.

There's an excitement in the room akin to the giddiness of political volunteers readying for a campaign. People are eager to mingle with others who feel as passionately as they do about co-living and want to spread its gospel. When the group conversation breaks into casual one-on-one chatter, it's nice to have support for co-living as a shared starting point. Unlike parents who don't get it, or coworkers who think communes are weird, everyone here is open to co-living, even if they're not living the lifestyle just yet.

But the vision of co-living presented here tonight can feel limited, even exclusive. For everyone here, co-living is a choice—and these are people who have many choices, from what restaurant to eat in to where to live. Many of the tech workers in the room chose their profession specifically because it offers the flexibility to get paid while they travel. They're not about to let conventional housing options lock them into a place or a way of life. "I've been so happy with the lifestyle that I'd like to live in a commune for the rest of my life," Morris says.

Morris, age thirty-two, has lots of peers settling into familiar patterns of domestic privacy. But she has no plans to follow them yet, and in the future if she does have children, she says she'd want to raise them in a communal lifestyle, co-parenting with her housemates. She sees no reason why the benefits of co-living she's already experienced—pooling resources, sharing chores, meeting new people, and helping each other out when sick or busy—wouldn't carry over when it comes to raising kids.

In other words, Morris believes communal living isn't just for affluent young nomads—it could work for just about everyone. If she's right, co-living could radically change housing as we know it.

NOT EVERYONE HAS the time, money, and initiative to build a Gramercy House. But thousands of other Americans are looking to buy—or, rather, rent—into a version of this lifestyle. They want activities after work, a nicely furnished living room, interesting housemates and occasional visitors, and outsourced housework. And they are willing to pay a premium—whether in money, privacy, space, or all of the above—for these amenities.

One of the drivers of this change is clear enough: personal and professional life has become more and more digital, and people crave in-person interaction. As an increasing percentage of the population lives alone, Americans aren't always finding that interaction easily.

Humans are a social species. We need strong relationships with other people, not only to avoid loneliness but simply to feel alive. We know this intuitively, and studies have confirmed that both the quantity and quality of social relationships affect mental health, health behavior, physical health, and mortality risk.[2] Those with unhealthy habits (like smoking or heavy drinking) but strong social ties exhibit lower mortality rates than those without strong social ties.[3] Families themselves once used to provide constant companionship—a full fifth of households in 1900 had seven or more persons—but today more people are living on their own or in small families, away from their relatives.[4] The old informal networks of religion, sports leagues, and other community groups that enabled social connection have frayed, if not entirely vanished. This is not a new trend—we have fretted about the lonely American at least since Robert Putnam's *Bowling Alone* was published in 2000. But not until recently has a generation of Americans sought to live in more communal environments.

Numbers—demographics and dollars—also explain the allure of co-living. The more than 83 million Americans born between 1982 and 2000 are waiting longer to get married and buying fewer homes.[5] While as of the first quarter of 2020 65.3 percent of people nationally own homes, just 37.3 percent of people aged under 35 do.[6] There is no single explanation for this shift, but the brokeness of millennials plays a big part. Only 22 percent of millennials are debt free, and 11 percent owe more than $100,000, which puts homeownership out of reach for many of them.[7] They're also more likely to live in cities than suburbs or rural areas. In cities, particularly coastal ones, housing costs are high and marriage before thirty is increasingly rare. A Pew study notes that 81 percent of millennials in Washington, DC, were not married; across the country, the share of households aged twenty to thirty-four that were married was just 37 percent in 2017, dropping from 45 percent as recently as 2000.[8]

The latest crop of young adults may not be getting married or buying real estate, but nonetheless many want high-quality housing and social experiences. For some, that means more sophisticated surroundings. A grimy collection of IKEA furniture and frustrating encounters with poorly matched roommates were once hallmarks of postcollegiate life, but in an age of heightened FOMO (fear of missing out) and Instagram feeds showing people living their #bestlife, many young people want stylish furniture, communal meals in dramatically sized shared dining rooms, and amenities like yoga classes or nightly activities. Co-living offers these savvy young people something akin to what H&M does for clothes or UberPool does for transportation—a proxy for luxury at lower cost.

Young and affluent consumers (the "work hard, play hard" constituency) spend most of their time at the office or on the town. Co-living simplifies their domestic expenses. Those who loathe dealing with laundry, pet care, utilities, or even food and drink have found that many co-living operators will take care of these tasks. For people who are so busy that they can't plan their weekends, or who suffer from decision paralysis, co-living community managers, sometimes called concierges, can take care of that too. Is this kind of supportive housing infantilizing young adults? Co-living residents might respond that this is a practical response to coping with seventy-hour workweeks without anyone to help with the rest of life's maintenance.

Other demographics find co-living appealing as well. Americans are nowadays more transient, for a variety of reasons. A full third of Americans work on a freelance basis. If current trends continue, the majority of American workers are expected to be freelancers by 2027. Some of those freelancers are digital nomads, like the computer programmer at Morris's gathering, whose profession is tied only to a laptop. Other Americans, particularly those over fifty, want housing that can flex as needed for a job shift, a divorce, or the next phase of life. For nomads by choice, freelancers, and people who want their housing to be more adaptable in response to life changes, co-living offers something like pay-as-you-go housing.

Saving money, living in more desirable areas, increasing flexibility, creating community, organizing lives: that's a lot of promises for co-living to fulfill. But there isn't a singular co-living model or experience. The residents, the style, and the rules change constantly. When I spoke with Claire Flurin in 2018, then the executive director of Co-Liv Lab, she said, "We're still at the beginning. Co-living is a new industry, even though people have been sharing houses forever." Indeed, even in the two years between when we spoke and when this book was published, co-living has become more varied as it has become more popular.

TO CHRIS BLEDSOE, a cofounder of the co-living company Ollie, the modern renter's various needs are "pain points." About a decade ago, Bledsoe's brother Andrew was a New York newbie who wanted to live in the center of all the restaurants, bars, parks, and transit but couldn't really afford his one-bedroom apartment. So he installed pressurized walls to subdivide the living room, adding two more bedrooms to the apartment. Craigslist advertisements for these tiny rooms got ninety responses in forty-eight hours. Soon Andrew had two new roommates, who were rarely home but paid enough rent that he was living for free in one of the country's most expensive housing markets.

The subdivision became a eureka moment for the brothers. Some people just wanted cheap access to the city, not necessarily a lot of space and not even necessarily privacy. The idea for Ollie was born. But installing pressurized walls in rental apartments around the city didn't exactly scale—and landlords wouldn't permit it either. The city had strict regulations on the size of rooms and apartments. For example, in a building constructed after 1955, a bedroom could be no less than 80 square feet, a living room no less than 150 square feet.[9] By these standards, Andrew's partitioned apartment wasn't even legal.

Then, in 2012, Mayor Michael Bloomberg launched a competition, called adAPT NYC, to design and construct a micro-apartment building prototype on a piece of city-owned land in the Kips Bay section of Manhattan. At the time, city regulations prohibited a building composed of only studios; for this project, the city relaxed restrictions on the size of units and the number of micro-units in one building. The winning proposal featured fifty-five units ranging in size from 260 to 360 square feet, and 40 percent of the units were set aside for military veterans using housing choice (Section 8) vouchers. Typically, developers wouldn't invest in this kind of project; there's more risk when all the units are the same size—not to mention undersize. It's easier to develop and then sell or rent a building with some two- or three-bedroom apartments to appeal to different customers with different price points. But with the city supporting the project, the prototype could show its merit and perhaps convince developers to consider micro-units in the future.

The project's developer, Monadnock Development, enlisted Ollie as a "micro-housing specialist" to operate the building, adding features such as a community manager who organizes yoga, dog walking, and dry-cleaning services for both the market-rate and subsidized units (all of which are provided at a lower price point for low-income tenants), as well as communal events like Sunday brunch and a 1920s murder mystery party.

The New York City project, now known as Carmel Place, launched Ollie's business with a proof of concept. Ollie then went on to partner with developers to operate three more projects: first, a 127-unit building in Pittsburgh catering to

Carnegie Mellon graduates working for Google and Uber, then a 297-unit building in Long Island City, New York, that opened in May 2018, and finally a 41-unit development in Newark, New Jersey. They have projects coming soon in Boston and Los Angeles.

"Housing has already been disrupted. The world just doesn't know it yet," Chris Bledsoe proclaims. "Because, if you're lucky, this is a product that takes three to four years to bring to market." Ollie's Long Island City project, ALTA+, opened after four years of negotiation and construction. "What we'll see four years from now is merely a reflection of where we are today. And what we'll see four years after that—that's what's really exciting."

Bledsoe sees Ollie's pipeline of projects as a part of a larger wave. Ollie is currently examining dozens of other projects across the country, with approximately three hundred beds each, and a handful of international ones. Developers who are building new construction or renovating old are seeking out Ollie's unique style of architectural and design services, programming, branding, and national network to transform mundane real estate projects into trendy co-living. Ollie also brings experience to the table: creating a co-living building is a tricky business, what with varying local zoning restrictions and the challenge of creating small but not cramped quarters—a skill that Ollie has mastered. Micro-units are far outside the wheelhouse of many developers used to old formulas of two-bedroom apartments with kitchens full of stainless steel appliances, cherry cabinets, and granite countertops. The number of inquiries and proposals from outside developers who want to partner with Ollie is "more than we have the bandwidth for," Bledsoe says.

Ollie's large-scale plans aren't an outlier. Other major co-living developers are equally ambitious. X Social Communities is the co-living department of real estate development company PMG. After twenty-five years in the traditional real estate business, with more than $6 billion in developments since its inception, PMG is now turning toward co-living. Brian Koles, a communications director there, cringes at the term co-living ("We call them social communities") but nonetheless notes that whatever this housing format is called, it's popular. X Social Communities, which are typically full of millennials who "aren't yet making six figures" already exist in Miami, Fort Lauderdale, and Chicago, and the company has approximately ten thousand beds in the works in major American cities within the next five years.

Starcity, a California co-living operator founded in 2016, announced its series B round of funding, totaling $30 million during the COVID-19 crisis in April 2020. Common—a provider of shared apartments in New York, Boston, and DC—has recently expanded to San Francisco, Chicago, Seattle, and Philadelphia. WeLive, also founded in 2016, still has only two communities to its name, in New York City and Arlington, Virginia. Plans to expand to Seattle fizzled after parent company WeWork's failed IPO in 2019.

The trend isn't limited to America or even to real estate companies. Mini, the British car manufacturer, began construction in 2018 to convert a former industrial building in Shanghai, turning the abandoned site into apartments, offices, and shared living spaces for its first community. The Collective, London's biggest co-living operator, pulled in a whopping $400 million in funding to expand further into the United Kingdom and enter the United States and Germany with a total of 4,500 new units.

All these new projects signal that developers are thinking co-living could be as popular in the future as luxury apartments have been in the last two decades. Koles notes that PMG moved into co-living because the luxury market was saturated and there was a shortage of housing stock aimed at people who make too much to be considered low-income but not enough to afford a traditional luxury apartment. The tight spaces and added number of tenants in co-living developments also mean more revenue per square foot. So far, the trend shows no sign of diminishing. "Once the lightbulb goes on for the developer and investor community, it doesn't go back off—it just stays on," Bledsoe tells me.

That said, developing a co-living space is more difficult than your typical residential project. Bledsoe likes to talk about "gatekeepers." There are government gatekeepers, who dictate which buildings can be built and how they should look, not to mention the zoning and building codes that need to be altered or adhered to. There are neighborhood gatekeepers, like community boards and civic associations, who can shut down new developments by withholding approval or pushing back against development alongside local government. Such NIMBY groups often fear potential effects on property values, safety, and parking. ("Innovation is fun, but in housing it means it's risky, and that can be a bad word in a lot of communities," Bledsoe says.)

A different type of risk can worry investors, whose funding ultimately determines what gets built. Debt investors in multifamily housing are extremely risk averse: they're looking for products that have the same returns and stability as government bonds. "They want to fund the same building that they funded last time. The problem is that if you do that over and over, you end up with a building made for the 1970s even though there have been seismic social shifts between 1970 and today," Bledsoe says.

Still, investors' conservatism seems to be giving way to a run on co-living at scale. Looking at the real estate landscape, this makes sense. The high end of markets from Sydney to Vancouver to New York have been sliding, sensing that international investment in luxury real estate may have already peaked. International instability—from Brexit to the Trump administration's nationalist policies to COVID-19—is deterring some international buyers from investing in luxury real estate. Co-living presents a new direction for developers and real estate investors who have run out of other options. If it can be proven profitable, you can bet it will make its mark on young people today.

Wasn't co-living supposed to be more Kumbaya than this?

OLLIE DOES HAVE an ethos, albeit one that sounds like an advertising slogan. The company has its "four Cs": convenience, comfort, cost savings, and community. While other major co-living operators may not have such a pithy statement of purpose, they're all catering to these broad concepts. Each such project pitches itself as offering some advantage, whether in terms of saving money or time, fostering a sense of community, or embracing style.

To see how these elements played out in reality, I visited Ollie's ALTA+ development in Long Island City, which is in the Queens borough of New York City. Tucked between elevated train tracks, a large railyard, and the westbound on-ramp of the Ed Koch Queensboro Bridge, ALTA+ is in a busy location, even by New York standards. Its green glass tower fits in with the dozens of new residential high-rises in the neighborhood, luring those willing to live in Queens, instead of tonier addresses in Brooklyn or Manhattan, at a smidge lower cost.

At first glance, ALTA+ looks like a regular apartment building. There's a lobby with seating areas (nothing that screams "community" about them) and a front desk with a doorman. The first sign that something is a little different is an ATM in the elevator bank, not exactly the warmest decor choice, but a nod to the convenience that co-living's all about. The hallways, with their dark rugs and walls, feel a bit like a hotel—sexy, modern, but a little anonymous.

The apartments lining these moody hallways come in three sizes—micro-studio, two-bedroom, or three-bedroom—but much of the design is uniform across different units. The apartments are white and bright, with bedroom windows framing views of the elevated subway trundling by. The largest three-bedroom is just 941 square feet, and every inch gets used. The shared kitchenette is streamlined with petite appliances; the table for three looks like a comfortable perch for one person with a laptop and coffee. The apartments force residents to re-think space and stuff—and pushes them to conclude that most Americans have way too much of both.

Through a partnership with Resource Furniture, a company that specializes in space-saving furnishings, the bedrooms come with specially designed Murphy beds that serve as love seats by day (WeLive also uses the same beds, which has made them unofficial symbols of the co-living movement). The beds can also fold up into the wall, but that leaves the bedroom with no seating. While residents can bring in their own furnishings, the condensed layouts discourage it. And residents are not allowed to take any of Ollie's provided furniture out. ALTA+'s design feels like a mix of East Germany and Marie Kondo, where life has been pared down to its essentials, for better or worse. In a cultural moment where the paradox of choice often paralyzes us and some tech folks eat Soylent and wear the same style T-shirt every day in the name of efficiency, there is something very on trend about the one-style-fits-all vibe of these dwellings.

In contrast with the tightly packed apartments, the shared spaces in the building are expansive. Residency comes with access to an enormous gym, lap pool, yoga studio, additional shared kitchen and dining space, and rooftop deck.

Bledsoe sees ALTA+ and similar projects as a natural reflection of social change. "[Micro-housing] just represents this shift, this evolution in society, which is the favoring of experience over stuff. And if you're not accumulating stuff, you don't need as much space to store it," he says. In New York at least, you're going to be cramped no matter what. Why not pare your square footage to the bone and get additional amenities in exchange?

One of those amenities is, allegedly, an authentic experience of a community, although paying for authenticity might seem like a contradiction in terms. Bledsoe tells the story of how the community manager at one Ollie property organized a ski trip. At the time, Ollie's website relied on stock images, so a photographer was hired to capture real residents having real fun. Bledsoe was worried that a photographer stalking tenants on the slopes would weird them out, but the opposite was true. All the residents wanted the photographer to capture "hero shots"—in advertising lingo—of their skiing exploits and generally document all the fun they had. To Bledsoe, this kind of performed community amounts to a huge shift in how to connect with potential customers.

"Today's consumer doesn't want to be marketed to. They want you to show them the experience, not tell them," Bledsoe says. He thought he was organizing events as a way to build community. But he came to realize that not only were these experiences enhancing connections among residents, but they were perfect marketing opportunities to show potential residents what living at Ollie was all about.

Is hiring a photographer to shoot glamorous stills of a group outing really authentic community connection? That might depend on your opinion of social media as a whole. But there's a case to be made that the current boom in co-living gets some of its DNA from reality TV shows, like *The Real World* and *Jersey Shore*, that millennials grew up watching. Those programs showed shared houses full of fun, sex, and drama. They also regularized constant outside surveillance. While the idea of inviting a professional photographer on your family vacation might seem invasive or overly image conscious to Generation Xers, it's much more normal to those born in the past thirty years.

I remained skeptical that these large co-living projects were really generating community, so I booked a stay at WeLive on Wall Street to investigate further. Located in a revitalized pocket of downtown Manhattan that teems with office workers during the day and young residents by night, this former office building has been thoroughly updated for its new uses. On the ground floor are trendy restaurants, including a vegetarian eatery and an ice cream shop that dishes up chocolate-covered-pretzel soft serve for $5 a pop. In the lobby, cheerful bass-heavy music pumps from unseen speakers as young people grab free lattes from the barista next to the check-in desk. (WeLive is located in the same building as a WeWork.) Unlike at ALTA+, this lobby feels lived in—people lost in laptops occupy the lounge furniture, and I expect to be greeted by someone more like a camp counselor than a building super. Instead, I meet a security guard wearing a T-shirt that says, "Live Better Together," who gives me a key and a pamphlet explaining WeLive. (I later learned that people who sign up for real leases get a warmer reception involving alcohol, a duffel bag, and other goodies.)

I check into my studio apartment, one of about two hundred units across twenty floors of private residential and shared common space. Though just as small as an Ollie apartment, the WeLive studio feels a bit more personal. ALTA+ consciously avoids a dorm feel, but WeLive embraces a more playful, collegiate vibe. There is a small selection of books—a biography of the poet Ted Hughes, Larry Kramer's satire *The American People: Volume I*—and a chalkboard in the kitchen to hash out ideas or leave notes to a roommate. Even the full-size bed built into a nook in the wall feels purposefully lighthearted. If ALTA+ appeals to the young adult who wants to be taken seriously, WeLive welcomes the one who isn't quite ready to grow up. Even some of the elevator banks emphasize this tone, decorated with sayings like "Don't forget ur keys" and "Don't forget ur wallet."

I dump my stuff and scout the communal spaces for evidence of community. There's a terrace overlooking the East River with two hot tubs, a "great kitchen" with free La Colombe coffee brewing all day, the laundry room with Ping-Pong and billiards, and a lounge. But the only people I encounter are alone with their laptops, either deeply focused on their work or longing for interaction. Admittedly, it can be hard to tell the difference. I feel a cynical satisfaction that the community message is just another marketing myth. Until I go to happy hour.

Every night from six to eight o'clock, WeLive serves up free alcohol in some form—mimosas, beer, cocktails. "Open bar" is too formal a term for this gathering. There are eight bottles of white and rosé, cups, a half-dozen residents, and me. The happy hour takes place in a small room the size of a hotel-suite kitchen, rather than one of the grand common spaces. It has low ceilings and low lighting, but with its just-off-the-elevators location, the bar never feels too secluded or serious. With six or seven of us standing around and sitting on bar stools, we have a hearty quorum.

My companions on this summer Monday night are five guys and one other woman, all in their early to midtwenties. Unlike the crowd at Gillian Morris's Gramercy House salon, who all dressed the part of sophisticated world travelers, this group is normcore in baggy jeans and T-shirts, with the occasional unironic baseball hat. The woman, an unpretentious dirty blonde I'll call Jane, encourages me to help myself to wine. (I have changed names to protect the privacy of people I met without the explicit purpose of reporting on them.) I explain I'm here to check out WeLive and see what a co-living space is like. Without any further prompting, the attendees offer themselves as exemplary WeLive residents.

Jane, a Canadian working in health care, has lived there for two years. When she moved to the United States she didn't have any credit, which made it hard for her to get a regular lease. She comments that the happy hours during the summer are less popular; in the winter there are usually more people— like twenty-plus. Perhaps disappointed with the turnout, she soon heads out. Two other young men take her place.

My fellow drinkers—all men now—occasionally sink into their cell phones when the conversation dries up. They all make the same jokes about the wine—"Rosé all day," "Frozé," "Rosé all the way"—but they admit to preferring it to the white wine.

Nirav, who works for American Express, tells me he's also been there for two years. Another resident, Jackson, was one of the first to move into the building with his partner before We-Live was even fully up and running. The guys are curious about me and better conversation partners than your average stranger at a bar, asking me about my life with genuine interest. When I ask them what they like about WeLive and why they ended up there, they're enthusiastic evangelizers. The convenience factor is huge: Not having to pick out carpet, furniture, or possessions in general. Not minding how much water or heat they use. "I've got my faucet running in my apartment right now, so I don't have to wait to turn it on," one of them jokes. It's great to live near work and grab free coffee on the way out the door. Obviously, events like happy hour and gym classes are perks.

They also talk about community, and I find myself thinking of *Cheers* or the movie *Diner*, where the same friends gather night after night and shoot the shit. Most of these guys have been at WeLive for months, if not years. While they mingle with plenty of short-timers like myself, they have a crew of semipermanent residents. A guy in his thirties enters with two dogs, and it's clear that no matter who comes off the elevator, the happy hour guys know them. They take some pride in being part of WeLive. It seems as if everyone has done shots with the infamous ex-CEO Adam Neumann on one of his visits to town. They emphasize another point: if they don't want to be social, they don't have to be. But if they want to go to the hot tub, they know they'll find someone interesting there.

Is WeLive a community for bros? Throughout my time there, I saw plenty of young women: one padding around in pajamas, another making eggs in a communal kitchen, a retiree who makes conversation in the elevator. Not everyone there is a young guy working in tech or finance. At the happy hour I meet Jonathan, a forty-two-year-old who is working on his memoir. Nirav identifies Jonathan as someone he'd never otherwise meet, were it not for WeLive. At a time when some people are having trouble meeting others who differ from them, there's at least the appearance of a good mix in this building. But like any self-selecting community, there is a shared identity, defined by being able to afford WeLive's high rents and being interested in its convenient lifestyle.

WHEN I WAS in my twenties, I was a freelancer and graduate student in New York who scoured Craigslist to find cheap furniture, attended art openings for their free wine and cheese, walked twenty minutes to the nearest affordable gym, and sometimes went without the internet to save money. In my first illegally sublet, rent-stabilized apartment, I suffered occasional panic attacks of loneliness and spent many nights lying in bed wondering if the strange sounds I heard were someone breaking through the three locks on my front door. Life would have been much easier if someone else set up the Wi-Fi and TV, cleaned my apartment once a week, and provided cool furnishings and pots and pans. It would have been comforting to grab a drink with neighbors in a communal space just outside my door. I definitely would have made it to the gym more often if it was just an elevator ride away.

But had communities like Ollie or WeLive existed back then, they would have been way beyond my budget. And they would have been at odds with the growing pride I took in my frugal lifestyle and self-sufficiency. While cost savings is pitched as one of Ollie's four Cs, the fact is that upmarket co-living developments' amenities come at a steep price. A 265-square-foot unit at Carmel Place in Manhattan costs $2,600 per month. A bedroom in a shared house at Common costs $1,350 per month, minimum. A studio at WeLive Wall Street is $3,000. Gramercy House costs $12,500 per month, split among six roommates. These rents are only cheap compared to amenity-filled, high-end rentals in desirable neighborhoods. Many co-living operators can credibly claim their units are cheaper than market rate once the bundled costs of utilities, insurance, and so on are factored in. But a true apples-to-apples comparison is impossible in a place like New York.

In researching New York City housing options, Claire Flurin of Co-Liv Lab found that almost one-third of New Yorkers have incomes too high to qualify for affordable housing but too low to meet the typical demands in a lease. (In New York, a landlord will often ask for proof of an annual income that is forty times the monthly rent amount. Then, to lease the apartment, you need first and last month's rent, plus a deposit and a broker's fee.) Flurin says that co-living's potential for affordability is in the idea of "unbundling the home." Instead of paying for an entire apartment, and having to cover expenses that you may not need, with co-living "you can buy a bed, or a bed and bathroom." In other words, why pay for a kitchen if you never use it?

But more often than not, this vision of cost savings through efficiency is still co-living's potential—not its reality. For co-living to meet its claims of revolutionizing how we live, it can't just be for rich yuppies. A few operators are moving into the low end of the co-living market. In Los Angeles, PodShare operates in five locations that offer bunk beds in a shared room for $50 a night, $280 a week, or $1,000 a month. Its twenty-nine-year-old founder Elvina Beck (who started the company with her father) makes first-person videos about ending loneliness and saving the world from climate change with more dense housing. Unlike the amenity-oriented marketing pitches of Ollie and WeLive, PodShare's approach is about embracing new social, environmental, and economic realities. It proudly appeals to "temps," "transitioners," and "travelers."

As PodShare's ethos posits, co-living could offer solutions to the affordable housing crisis, the difficulty of Americans' round-the-clock work schedules, and a growing loneliness epidemic. But to truly broaden the target market for co-living beyond the affluent and luxury minded, for-profit developers will need incentives to forgo some of the luxury amenities that have made co-living a profitable option.

Co-living has the potential to be a cheaper housing option, but only if people are paying for a bedroom and little else. Jenny Schuetz, a housing expert at the Brookings Institution, says, "If you think about the early twentieth-century boardinghouse, people were just renting a bedroom and a shared bathroom and kitchen. The more things you take out of the individual apartment, the cheaper the apartment should be. If you're aiming this at a very high level of services and amenities for the building, the individual apartments aren't going to get that much cheaper." Even a newly constructed boardinghouse won't be cheap, simply because construction costs are so high. To get co-living to work for average renters, the current branding needs to shift toward efficiency rather than convenience.

Though the current crop of co-living projects trends high-end, there is a sense that these developments are pushing cities (and citizens) to question their long-held assumptions that shared housing is undesirable to everyone except college students and seniors. Co-living has taken off at the same time that affordable housing has grown scarce. Taking a page from the Bloomberg administration's adAPT NYC playbook, cities such as New York and Philadelphia are working to develop new zoning codes for shared-housing prototypes, with an eye toward affordability and demographics that desire new housing options. To incorporate more shared living, city governments will have to rethink codes and regulations that forbid, for example, a building with ten separate bedrooms, two bathrooms, and one kitchen. In Philadelphia, there are an estimated five hundred boardinghouses operating illegally. Rezoning and regulatory reform could enable these establishments to exist legally, hundreds of units could come out of the shadows, and residents would be protected by regulations that ensure the safety of these buildings. That being said, part of the reason co-living has flourished at the high end is precisely because of its clientele. "The stigma of SROs has very little to do with the structure type and everything to do with who lived in SROs. We stigmatize housing that's primarily occupied by low-income people, people of color, formerly homeless people," says Schuetz. If co-living goes low-end, public appetite for it might fade quickly. "Do I see single-family, high-end neighborhoods zoned to allow co-living? I really doubt it," Schuetz says.

A long history of exclusionary patterns in the history of American housing bolsters Schuetz's skeptical take. But we may not have the choice to silo ourselves by class or other demographics in the future. Density and scale loom large in a crowded future, along with sustainability concerns. Co-living could offer help on both fronts. Starcity claims that it houses three times the typical number of residents in its communities, and it's vividly apparent that a 941-square-foot three-bedroom at Ollie could easily fit in a spacious one-bedroom at the same square footage. Co-living's density and shared amenities could also alleviate the environmental impact of housing. With its focus on communal space and sharing, co-living refutes the standard association of stuff with "making it." As young people have delayed buying cars in favor of ride shares and bike lanes, fewer cars are polluting and less wealth is lost to lease payments, insurance premiums, and repairs. Imagine that same effect multiplied across beds, sofas, lamps, pots, and pans—items that routinely line city streets on trash day—and the environmental and economic benefits start to seem very real. If a co-living space is located in a city with public transportation infrastructure, it could also drive the density needed to make more train or bus service viable.

Co-living could cause cities to rethink the role that outdated zoning plays in their affordability and environmental crises. Instead of having minimum size requirements for apartments, what if cities had maximum size regulations that outlawed, for example, four-thousand-square-foot single-family homes? That's an unlikely scenario, but the very existence of co-living poses a head-scratcher: If a person cannot afford more than two hundred square feet, why are many locales legally preventing them from living in such a small space?

Finally, co-living could help people find friends and a sense of belonging—particularly young people born since 1990, who, according to a study by the health insurer Cigna, have the highest rates of loneliness of any generation living today—but only if it doesn't turn community into a luxury good.[10] It's no surprise there's high demand for co-living's pay-for-community model, given that young people are using apps like Tinder and Bumble not for dating but for finding friends, and Facebook's events feature to figure out what to do in their spare time. But where does that leave everyone who can't afford the built-in social network of Ollie or WeLive? As more people delegate their social lives to co-living managers and private spaces, it might pull attention and resources away from sites and styles of public community. Much like the way gyms siphoned away rec center users and Amazon helped lure people from the library, co-living at scale could make private socializing something people aspire to—more popular than going out to a park, a bar, or a cultural event and bumping up against strangers.

Likewise, it's imperative that the outsourcing inherent in co-living not be used to create an ever-greater buffer between those who can pay to solve their problems and those whose jobs and lives revolve around drudgery. One imagines that a co-living lifestyle could widen the gulf between haves and have-nots and add to the insularity and sense of entitlement that keep the affluent in a bubble. But by steering spending away from stuff and square footage and into experiences, there's the alternative potential that co-living could boost service industries that employ local people, rather than furniture companies (who mostly automate or offshore their labor).

There's also the potential for co-living to help address some of the gender inequality within the home. One survey found that 25 percent of couples divorce due to "disagreements over housework," and a working paper by Harvard Business School and the University of British Columbia found that "those who spent more money on timesaving services were more satisfied with their relationships, in part because they spent more quality time with their partners." Could a style of co-living targeted at married couples actually save relationships or ease the strain of raising children?

If co-living is only marketed to the affluent, it stands to worsen the class stratification, privatization, and delayed adulthood that have slowly become ingrained in American culture. But if taken seriously as a new style of living for all kinds of people, it's hard to imagine how it couldn't benefit society.

IN 2018, NEW York City launched a request for expressions of interest around a program that would demonstrate how shared living could help create more affordable housing. A year later, the program, called ShareNYC, announced three demonstration projects that would collectively create three hundred affordable "housing opportunities" in distinct locations around the city.

A ten-story, thirty-six-unit project in East Harlem will be filled with referrals from the shelter system. Like traditional co-living, the apartments will be furnished and rent will include all utilities and amenities. Built by a neighborhood development corporation, Ascendant Neighborhood Development, in partnership with the Ali Forney Center, the project will host programs that teach life skills and offer coaching.

Another project—to be built by a major co-living developer, Common—will house 253 units across two eight-story buildings. The project will aim to be truly mixed income, with just one-third reserved for market-rate rents. One of the buildings will feature grand common spaces, such as a recreation room and dining area, while the other will have more intimate shared spaces.

Finally, the third project will be operated by PadSplit, a company typically focused on sharing single-family residences, in collaboration with Cypress Hill Local Development

Corporation. Here, the challenge is to rehabilitate an eleven-unit SRO to modern standards. All three demonstration projects also have green features that lower the buildings' carbon footprint.

New York's Department of Housing Preservation and Development not only selected the projects but is providing public financing and zoning easements to enable their completion. The department will also learn what works and doesn't, what kinds of zoning changes will be needed to accommodate co-living, and how shared living can actually create more density and affordability.

This effort hints at co-living's true potential to create density and affordability. Through public and private collaboration, we might see co-living targeted at specific users who would benefit greatly from shared spaces, community building, and lower rents.

CO-LIVING HAS CAPTIVATED people and developers because it is a new frontier: its significance in society is not yet understood; its potential for good or for profit has not been fully realized. Is it just a new marketing strategy for high-end apartments or a genuine attempt to create more community in anonymous cities? Is it posh, hotel-style living or ultra-minimalism? Is it living lean and mean or just a different breed of bourgeois? Is it even new or just a new branding campaign for an old style of living? Is it a passing upmarket trend, or could it make our cities greener, friendlier, and more accessible to all?

The truth is that it's all of the above, or it can be. There's no certainty here, only massive potential to change the way buildings are built and lives are lived. Despite healthy skepticism about whom the boom benefits and how, shared housing as a mainstream style of living would radically reorient the country's housing market and experience of adulthood. Most dramatically, it could change how Americans view the investment of housing. After World War II, home sizes increased throughout the country. "Homes became McMansions," Chris Bledsoe notes. "Not that people needed all that space, but homes became a status symbol and also a piggy bank. A place to park wealth. A renter is not getting a rebate check back at the end of the month for space they're not utilizing."

Bledsoe is talking about nothing less than a shift in how—or whether—people build wealth and what their aspirations are. For the past forty years, the American vision of the good life has largely hewed to the dreams of baby boomers, who have long coveted sprawling houses full of tchotchkes. On the surface, this domestic paradise seems wholesome; but when accounting for its economic, social, and environmental consequences, it's a lot more pernicious. It's the mess that co-living could get us out of: Why did housing have to become so expensive, so isolating, so bad for our health and the planet?

Gillian Morris of Gramercy House found a way to recreate her nontraditional upbringing in a practical, bespoke present, and she and a small but influential peer group are creating new traditions of their own. In 2020, she found herself living in a communal house in San Juan and is looking for a property to build a new one. Companies like Ollie, Starcity, and Common are seeing if this vision can scale. Governments and markets seem to be slowly catching on and partnering with co-living operators on affordable housing. All of this reflects a revision of the American Dream. For many people, an enviable Instagram feed is just as important as a white picket fence; breaking bread with neighbors is more satisfying than eating alone in a formal dining room. This is a trend that has ramifications way beyond housing and has already disrupted other industries like clothing and tourism. Millennials' social media feeds full of selfies and their preferences for short-term experiences over stability and ownership are often framed as vapid in comparison to past norms—which prioritized marriage and settling down in a single-family home to raise a nuclear family—but these trends are surprisingly democratic and, influencers aside, not necessarily consumption oriented. It's clear that millennials are looking at their lives for their present value and their ability to bring joy and connect with people. In co-living, they have found a way to do that without homeownership's downside of protecting wealth by exclusion. I'll drink a glass of rosé to that.

CHAPTER FIVE
SMALL IS BEAUTIFUL

BURLINGTON, VERMONT, IS NOT the kind of place one imagines when talking about the country's housing crisis. A quaint city of around 42,000 people located just forty-five miles south of the border from Canada, Burlington isn't facing the same kinds of pressures from foreign buyers that drive up housing costs in New York, and it doesn't have the huge number of tech jobs drawing thousands of highly paid buyers to the Bay Area. It's a leafy, lefty college town with a downtown pedestrian commons and the first Ben & Jerry's store.

But like in many other academic hubs such as Ithaca, New York, or Ann Arbor, Michigan, faculty, staff, and student demand for quality housing near campus has driven up housing prices beyond what average local salaries can bear. Vermont senator Bernie Sanders was mayor there in the 1980s and notably supported the formation of a local community land trust, a kind of public-private entity that ensures affordability by allowing people to own their home but lease the land it sits on from the trust. When homeowners sell their properties, they reap only a portion of the increase in value while the trust retains the rest.

Even with the Champlain Housing Trust, which some call the "most successful in the country," Burlington is facing a housing affordability crisis.[1] For Ehrin Lingeman, a twenty-five-year-old who moved to the area after graduating college and serving in the Peace Corps, finding housing that met her budget wasn't easy. Rents were typically $750 at the low end for a room in a house, and a studio was around $1,200 to $1,500—the kind of prices you might find in a city with high salaries to match rent costs. Lingeman supports herself as a farm educator and food sustainability specialist, and even when splitting rent with her partner, Raul, money was tight.

A few years ago, she learned that one of her students was looking to rent a small house on the edge of her property. At just 324 square feet, the house had everything Lingeman and her partner needed—living, dining, bedroom, and bathroom—and was beautifully crafted, and set on wheels to boot. Rent came out to less than $1,000. "It's pretty incredible," Lingeman says with an easy laugh.

Although Lingeman might humbly disagree, she is a trendsetter. Whether by choice or by force, a growing number of Americans are living in tiny homes. The humble mobile home (officially known as "manufactured housing," per a 1976 Department of Housing and Urban Development safety act) has been reincarnated to accommodate a new generation. Much as SROs have been reimagined as co-living, manufactured housing is undergoing a revamp.

There are a few differences between today's tiny homes and mobile or manufactured homes. First and foremost, manufactured housing is what it sounds like: factory built using industrial processes. Today's tiny homes may be mass-produced or, as in Lingeman's case, hand built. While mobile homes are associated with financial hardship, tiny homes are often framed as being desirable, born less out of survival than a do-more-with-less philosophy that enables individuals, couples, and even families with children to live large in less square footage. Advocates of tiny homes flaunt their minimalism and their aesthetic punch. In other words, the distinction is mostly a marketing ploy.

While mainstream America looks down on manufactured housing, it loves tiny homes. HGTV had not one, but two shows dedicated to tiny houses. The website for *Tiny House, Big Living* describes tiny houses as a "daydream for most people—but the intrepid folk who live in itty-bitty homes have a thing or two to teach the rest of us about living the good life and making the most of what we've got." Trendy mattress brand Allswell now manufactures fancy tiny houses selling for $100,000. The company touts its "tiny home that makes a huge style statement" on its website, claiming, "This smartly chic abode proves small is the new big. Its superb space utilization, sophisticated finishes, and exhaustive list of features (including two Allswell mattresses) stylishly underscore the fact that a luxe experience can indeed come in a little package."[2] Small is the new big, minimalism the new luxury.

The gentrification of the manufactured home might sound silly, or worse. But it has been critical to overcoming the stigma of small and impermanent (aka mobile) housing. Manufactured housing was until fairly recently seen as the option of last resort for people in suburban or rural contexts. Now tiny homes are seen as entry-level housing for low-paid professionals and young people with debt. Cities like Seattle and Detroit are deploying them in tiny-home villages as shelter for people who might otherwise be homeless. As a result, tiny homes are turning into big business.

Perhaps the most common use for a tiny house is as an add-on to a single-family home—an opportunity to take advantage of extra space in the backyard. Why have a lawn when you could generate income with a small rental property, or house relatives while preserving some privacy and independence for all involved?

That's Lingeman's case, though her living situation is technically illegal per Burlington's zoning code. Her home is also visible from the street, and if someone wanted to call in a code violation, they could. But, according to Lingeman, "Burlington's community is really receptive to this lifestyle." When the city hosted a housing summit in the summer of 2019 to address its affordability crisis, Burlington vowed to make it easier to build such backyard cottages, technically known as accessory dwelling units, as one of the five critical ways it intends to address its affordable housing shortage. Cities from Portland to Austin are passing legislation that rids the zoning code of too many restrictions on ADUs, in an effort to encourage homeowners to create them. In cities with older housing stock, like Philadelphia and New York, new zoning revisions encourage homeowners to create ADUs by carving out in-law suites or basement apartments in existing homes.

The potential for this type of home to fulfill an array of twenty-first-century housing needs has made it a favorite among a diverse group, from affordable housing advocates and local politicians to venture-capital-backed start-ups, mobile home manufacturers, and interior design enthusiasts. Whether as primary residences or ADUs, tiny homes are going to be a big trend in the coming decades.

BIG ISN'T ALWAYS better. For decades, the median size of a newly constructed home has ballooned, but trends suggest that it may have already peaked. While the average size of a newly constructed single-family home was just 1,000 square feet in 1950, it reached 2,687 square feet in 2015. In the five years since, the size of new homes has continuously fallen, now down to 2,511 square feet.[3] In 2017, the median lot size of a new single-family detached home was just 8,560 square feet, or under one-fifth of an acre, the smallest size since housing observers started keeping track.[4] It may just be that Americans are finally ready to downsize.

Small homes are a growing segment of the urban real estate market, with some 53 percent of people surveyed by the National Association of Home Builders (NAHB) saying they would consider moving to a home of six hundred square feet or less.[5] A 2017 Trulia survey showed that 60 percent of people whose living space was larger than two thousand square feet would actually prefer to live in a smaller home if they had to move.[6]

As the size of the single-family home increased throughout the twentieth century, the size of the household occupying all that space continuously decreased. Today, it's still on the decline, down to an average of just 2.6 people, and 28 percent of people live alone. Yet single individuals still have to pay the same housing costs as couples or families. With the average price of an apartment in hot markets like San Francisco at $3,700 per month according to RENTCafé, there are many people who cannot afford more than two hundred or three hundred square feet of private space, and, therefore, are the perfect market for tiny homes.[7]

At the same time, a huge segment of the housing market—baby boomers—is downsizing. Saddled with the family-size houses they raised their children in and the high cost of property taxes and upkeep, boomers are seeking out smaller homes and apartments. Some are looking to move closer to family—even into an ADU in their children's backyards—as a way to plan for their retirement.

On the supply side, many homeowners are interested in offsetting increases in the cost of living by building an ADU in their backyard or garage. Nowadays, people are interested in monetizing excess capacity—whether by taking on an Uber shift or renting a spare bedroom on Airbnb—and a part of that trend are the thousands of people creating backyard cottages and garage conversions to generate additional income with what was once wasted space.

Finally, city governments like Burlington are seeking ways to address housing shortages, but they don't have the funding to create more public housing or the political backing to build large, multifamily affordable housing projects. Enabling and encouraging private homeowners to build their own additional units is seen by many local governments as a way to add housing stock without much cost or change to the character of neighborhoods.

All of these conditions have created a very large market for tiny homes and ADUs. Banks are finally jumping in, looking for ways to finance these dwellings. As public, private, and civic-sector players hope to take advantage of this newfound niche, they're bringing tiny to the masses.

THE TWEE TERM "tiny homes" belies the seriousness of the trend toward smaller homes and the need for housing that fills this niche. Despite the fast-growing appeal of smaller and more affordable housing, not many of these houses exist. Just 2 percent of homes sold in New York City and San Francisco were under five hundred square feet.[8] And only 9 percent of new single-family "home starts" (the beginning of construction or permits pulled) are manufactured housing.[9]

Up until now, developers have not been incentivized to build small. Given that a developer's primary costs are land, utility hookups, and a construction crew, there's little incremental cost to building a 3,000-square-foot house instead of a 1,500-square-foot house. The reason the average size of a house has risen over the past half century isn't because people necessarily want all that extra space. Rather, developers are like restaurateurs who dish out large portions and charge more for them. The bigger the house, the higher the list price. Developers will add more bedrooms and bathrooms—or, even better, home offices and playrooms that require little additional infrastructure—so long as prices will bear it.

Small also carries stigma, especially when small houses are densely arranged. The occasional three-hundred-square-foot house is cute; if tucked away in a backyard, it can hardly offend anyone. But most communities have banned building small homes in any consistent, dense arrangement. Even the cutest commune of tiny houses will inevitably be compared with a trailer park and the unfortunate socioeconomic stigma associated with it; a building zoned for micro-apartments quickly gets dubbed a "dorm" or "hotel" in the media.

But the primary reason new small houses or apartments aren't being built in larger quantities is that, in many places, zoning and neighborhood regulations have made them illegal. In suburban contexts, homeowner associations often require a minimum-size house, in an effort to guarantee some uniformity to the neighborhood and keep prices relatively high. As the average house size has increased, these minimums have increased too—so that 1,500 square feet is often the smallest allowable size of new standalone home construction. In dense, urban contexts, zoning codes will allow for some studio apartments in a building with a mix of other apartment sizes. But many codes will not allow developers to construct buildings made solely of micro-apartments—typically, apartments of 350 square feet or less—by right, which is to say without getting approval from a zoning board and neighborhood association. This makes developers much less likely to take these projects on, due to the potential for neighborhood pushback and associated delays. Finally, because only a few micro-apartment buildings have been constructed, there's little investor confidence in these projects and developers find it hard to get them financed.

For all these reasons, small houses are still an oddity, mainly existing only when they've been grandfathered into neighborhoods. But more recently, affordable housing advocates, entrepreneurial developers, architects, and politicians have found that communities can address housing affordability concerns and better match housing to today's demographics by building small homes, whether as apartments, primary homes, or ADUs.

CALIFORNIA IS A state well-known for its sprawling, suburban communities. It's also home to some of the country's least affordable cities and counties. The median monthly housing cost for California homeowners with mortgages is 47 percent higher than the national average.[10] The National Low Income Housing Coalition estimates that there is a shortage of more than one million rental units that are affordable and available for extremely low-income people.[11] Not surprisingly, homelessness is on the rise in many counties in the state. In one stark example, between 2018 and 2019 homelessness spiked by a full 50 percent in Kern County, where Bakersfield is located.[12]

Los Angeles County is seeing a rise in its homeless population as well. Its homeless count was 58,936 in 2019, an increase of 12 percent over the previous year.[13] At the same time, the city's stock of old, courtyard housing and bungalows is losing out to luxury developments. In areas like Venice Beach, once known for tiny surfer shacks, newly constructed three-thousand-square-foot manses that sell for over $2 million are now the norm. As a result, the need for affordable housing is felt across economic strata. Nearly everyone is feeling pinched.

Dana Cuff has been studying the potential of ADUs to revolutionize Los Angeles's housing and bring affordability and sustainability to the city for more than a decade. An energetic sixty-something with a white-blonde bob of hair, Cuff is director of cityLAB, an architecture and urban planning think tank situated in UCLA's department of Architecture and Urban Design.

More than fifteen years ago, for its very first initiative in 2006, the lab asked teams of recent graduates from programs in real estate, architecture, and planning, What's one law that affects the production of market-rate housing you would change to make housing more affordable? One team identified the laws governing ADUs. They presciently argued that changing the laws that restricted the production of ADUs would unleash an enormous opportunity to build small-scale but pervasive affordable housing.

The scale was key: large, multifamily affordable housing projects are often unwanted in low-income areas or fought tooth and nail in wealthier neighborhoods. They're also complicated to build, often requiring funding from competitive tax-credit programs that add time and expense to the process. Developing ADUs could potentially offer the same number of housing units—or more—when spread across the city with less cost to the taxpayer and less agita in the neighborhood.

In retrospect, this elegant solution to create more housing without the expense, red tape, and concerns about the character of a neighborhood "seemed so obvious," Cuff says. According to Cuff, Los Angeles has roughly five hundred thousand single-family properties, many with backyards or garages that could be converted to housing. And, she says, the city already has thousands of unpermitted ADUs.

But at the time, only a few hundred ADUs were being legally built statewide. Cuff found that, of the half-million single-family lots in the city, approximately 80 percent were restricted "by a couple of arcane legislative regulations that everyone agreed were no longer relevant." For example, there were still restrictions in place that accommodated fire-safety equipment from the early twentieth century, despite the fact that such equipment was no longer used. The lack of a standard lot in LA meant that there was no uniform way to build an ADU. "Each one is like a fingerprint," Cuff says. This meant that there was no clear way to efficiently manufacture an ADU that would get cheaper at scale. Finally, the biggest obstacle was the requirement that the ADU have one or two dedicated parking spaces.

For decades, there has been a fair amount of local opposition to encouraging Los Angeles homeowners to build in their backyards. Cuff and colleagues would take drafts of potential legislation to LA councilmembers, encouraging zoning reform related to ADUs. Typically, councilmembers would initially respond with enthusiasm and support. But inevitably a local NIMBY group would pressure the council to reject the changes. In hindsight, Cuff assigns some of the councilmembers' reluctance to champion reforms to the fact that "it wasn't exactly clear what a resource backyards might be for affordable housing." Not even Cuff would have believed how homeowners would embrace building ADUs once the laws were changed.

Her first inkling that there was a lot of pent-up demand came from local meetings about changing ADU legislation. While the NIMBYs in the crowd were always the loudest, after every meeting there would be a handful of people who would discreetly approach Cuff in person or over email, asking, "How can I build one of these?"

In 2016, Cuff's state assemblyman, Richard Bloom, reached out to her asking for help with crafting new affordable housing legislation. Cuff pulled together a band of advisers, including city planner Jane Blumenfeld, who—as a creative policy wonk and, later, a cityLAB staffer—became Cuff's strongest partner in thinking through ways to encourage ADUs. Then Cuff got an email out of the blue from another group working completely independently on similar legislation with a state senator in Northern California. The two teams—all women—formed a coalition to create two separate but identical pieces of legislation to change the requirements that governed parking, utilities, and size. The bills, sponsored by Bloom and state senator Bob Wieckowski, passed in 2016 and became law in January 2017. "And it has been like opening a floodgate ever since," Cuff says.

CUFF IS NOT exaggerating; there is a genuine frenzy throughout California to build ADUs. Perhaps nowhere is there more urgency than in Los Angeles. In 2016, before California's legislation changed, only 257 ADUs were permitted. In 2017, that number jumped to 3,818.[14] In 2018, there were more than 4,000 permitted.[15] It's an astonishing figure when one considers that municipal authorities tend to add just a few hundred affordable housing units per year.

Given the economic dimension of LA's housing crisis, the relevant question is this: Will the ADUs be affordable to low- and moderate-income residents? Not necessarily. Just look at Vancouver, a city that legalized and encouraged ADUs in 2010, years before any of its peers on the West Coast. Called "laneway houses" instead of ADUs, there were about two thousand such structures built in Vancouver between 2010 and 2016.[16] But in many cases, these homes aren't geared toward low- or even moderate-income households. Rather, they're posh and profitable rentals, Airbnbs, or extra housing for visitors or relatives. In some cases, they're built to maximize the value of an already expensive property. ADUs may have added overall supply and density to Vancouver's residential neighborhoods, but they hardly staved off its affordable housing crisis.

So how could a city like Los Angeles address affordability through ADUs? Simply building more of them wouldn't necessarily help. But Helen Leung, a planner and policy wonk who once served as a planning deputy for Eric Garcetti's council district before he became Los Angeles's mayor, had an idea.

Leung is one of the co–executive directors of LA-Más, an architecture and policy nonprofit founded in 2012 with the mission of helping low-income and underserved communities "shape their future through policy and architecture." She speaks with a gravity and precision that convey how long and hard she's thought about LA's housing and how to improve it.

She grew up in the Frogtown neighborhood, a working-class part of the city that is rapidly gentrifying. Frogtown sits near the Los Angeles River—once an eyesore or, at best, a forgotten sliver of pseudo-nature, but which is now quickly becoming a Frank Gehry–planned attraction. Leung lived with her immigrant parents in a single-family home long before the neighborhood was trendy. Now that Frogtown is desirable, Leung's family could cash out and leave. Except, where could they go? In gentrifying cities like LA, the only option is to move to a cheaper, less desirable neighborhood.

Leung's family was asset rich but cash poor, a predicament common to many immigrants in LA. How could they afford the rising taxes and amenities of their neighborhood without moving? How could they ensure that the area still welcomed working-class immigrants, not just high-income newcomers?

While engaging in conversations with residents in Frogtown and neighborhoods like it, Leung found that many people wanted housing affordability, but "not the typical affordable housing, which is usually large-scale, high-density units." Leung talks about how many of her school classmates lived in garages that had been converted to apartments; it was another kind of ADU that served as naturally occurring affordable housing.

Leung and her LA-Más partner, architect Elizabeth Timme, began investigating ADUs as a potentially explosive housing opportunity. In a 2015 exhibit at the Los Angeles Architecture and Design Museum called *Shelter: Rethinking How We Live in Los Angeles*, Leung and Timme laid out a case for what ADUs could do for a neighborhood in terms of infrastructure, affordability, and density.

They also realized that if homeowners were going to go through all the time and trouble to build an ADU, not to mention the expense, many would be motivated to maximize their return on that investment and rent the ADU out at maximum profit (or use it for other benefits, such as housing family). Although many people were interested in renting out an ADU at an affordable rate—wanting to do their part in helping the city overcome its housing crisis—they still would require some kind of incentive to go through the construction process.

The incentive that Leung and Timme thought they could offer wasn't a straightforward financial subsidy, but, in a word, support. Homeowners needed someone to hold their hand through the process. Someone to help with finding a contractor, filing permits, and finding renters. So Leung and Timme pitched a pilot project to the City of Los Angeles. They would administer the project through their nonprofit, LA-Más. Leung knew how the city worked and had a network of contacts from her years serving Eric Garcetti. She was able to tap Councilmember Gil Cedillo for some modest funding to launch the program, and in partnership with the Bloomberg Innovation Team (a Bloomberg-funded consulting practice embedded in the LA mayor's office), LA-Más embarked on finding a family and a home that could serve as a guinea pig for developing an affordable ADU.

With this initial ADU, Leung sought to understand four things. First, could ADUs be designed contextually? Many ADU providers will convince you that any old rectangle will work with any old site. To make their business model work, one size must fit all. But that is often far from the truth. Backyards are made of different shapes and have different slopes. To take advantage of sunlight in one direction or privacy in another, ADUs would ideally respond to their context. Leung sought to create a small set of ADU templates that were nimble enough to be adjusted to the context of each property.

Second, could the construction cost be affordable? Leung knew that lots of Angelenos built unpermitted ADUs because they couldn't afford quality design and construction. So she found a nonprofit contractor who was invested in doing good work at a reasonable cost. With the right contractor, Leung could also offer the property owner an all-in cost for the ADU without worrying about overruns that could jeopardize the project.

Third, could a new financial product help ADUs scale? Like many homeowners seeking to build an ADU, the pilot participants Leung found were middle class but didn't have enough equity in their home to access traditional home-equity products. Genesis Bank, a local community development financial institution (CDFI) financed a construction loan for these cases, giving a glimpse of what would be required for underwriting ADUs.

Finally, how could this project inform policy? With the city as a partner, there was great potential for the project to inform how the city would approach ADUs, not only as a housing typology but as a source of affordable housing. Leung wanted to create a program that would require homeowners participating in it to rent their ADUs to HUD housing choice voucher (Section 8) tenants for five years. After that term, they could rent the unit at market rate. Hopefully some would continue to rent to Section 8 tenants, if only because the rent is guaranteed by vouchers. There would be no deed restriction, meaning that there was no way to force homeowners to do what they promised. But Leung felt this was the best shot at generating truly affordable ADUs. If ADUs wouldn't really get more affordable through scale, then Leung wanted to think about affordability "less in the sense of its construction cost, than that it could be rented affordably."

In 2018, LA-Más launched the Backyard Homes Project. Pitched as, "We build you a backyard home. You rent it affordably for 5 years," the project enables homeowners to partner with LA-Más for considerable pro-bono or low-cost help building an ADU in exchange for a restriction on whom the ADU is rented to. "It's hard for your average homeowner to be an amateur developer and we wanted to take those risks away," says Leung.

What LA-Más brings to the table is considerable. The organization serves as the architect, hires the nonprofit general contractor, and brings two financial partners (a credit union and a CDFI), who created a new financial product that takes an existing mortgage plus the cost of ADU construction and refinances the whole thing ("it's like a non-predatory cash out refi"). LA-Más then bundles all the hard and soft costs together so that, for example, they can charge $180,000 for a six-hundred-square-foot ADU.

The catch (if you want to call it that) is that the homeowners become Section 8 landlords for five years. "We know there's stigma around that," Leung says. On the other hand, the housing authority guarantees that rent gets paid. LA-Más has received a lot of interest from homeowners who feel a civic duty to provide affordable housing. Here again, LA-Más has built a supportive network to make the Section 8 process easy for landlords and tenants. For example, LA's housing department and the nonprofits St. Joseph Center and LA Family Housing provide resources for finding good tenants, and a housing-rights center trains landlords on particularly addressing the needs of Section 8 tenants. LA-Más has also anticipated that some landlords will want to outsource property management and partnered with a company on that.

So far almost two hundred people have applied to be part of the program. For Leung, that's an indication of real demand for this kind of project. But despite those hundreds of applicants, only two dozen are in the pipeline, and COVID-19 has thrown into question how many of those homeowners will move forward. LA-Más only has one completed ADU to show for it, the city's pilot project, which took two years to get built. LA-Más's program shows great opportunity to create affordable housing, but it also exemplifies just how hard it is to create market-oriented solutions that provide affordable housing at scale.

SCALE IS A term that the tech industry loves to use. The housing crisis in California may have been caused in part by the tech industry, with its fast-paced job growth and outsize salaries.

Now, the tech and start-up communities are hoping to come to the rescue. After all, housing is one sector that could benefit from tech's fixation on scale. Many entrepreneurs have rushed to create start-ups that will profit off this new market, claiming they can create housing faster and cheaper with new technology.

The company Cover claims to design a custom home for your backyard in just three days. They'll take care of zoning research, design, and permitting, seamlessly delivering a home. ICON out of Austin claims that "housing doesn't have to be a crisis" on its website. The company has built the first 3D-printed home and partnered with the nonprofit New Story to 3D print homes for communities around the world grappling with homelessness, natural disasters, and humanitarian crises.

Small in size, ADUs can be easily prefabricated and shipped to the owner. Silicon Valley entrepreneurs are salivating over the prospect of making money and solving the housing crisis at the same time. They pitch their prefab ADUs as innovative because they're both constructed off-site and can be purchased via the internet. If you can buy a Tesla by pointing and clicking, why shouldn't you be able to buy a three-hundred-square-foot home for about the same price?

But technology may not offer the cost or time savings that people have imagined. Allison Arieff is a San Francisco–based contributor to the *New York Times* op-ed page, and if you follow her Twitter feed you know she tends to be skeptical of Silicon Valley culture. Nearly twenty years ago, she wrote a book, *Prefab*, that ignited a spark of enthusiasm for small prefabricated homes, so much so that trendsetting modern home magazines like *Dwell* (which she once edited) began designing and selling premade homes.

Aside from the flashy websites that make buying an ADU sexy and compelling, Arieff sees nothing new here. "If you looked at the back issues of any architecture magazine from 2005 to 2010, there were fifty companies making these exact same claims," she says of the cyclical ambition to both provide cheap housing and solve the affordable housing crisis. Prefab has long been a darling of the twentieth-century architecture community, from Frank Lloyd Wright to Louis Kahn. It has also been a favorite of profit-minded producers: in the first four decades of the twentieth century, Sears sold through its catalog some seventy thousand homes that customers would construct from a kit of parts.[17]

But what about those websites showing little modern houses you could just imagine being airlifted into a backyard? Not much innovation there either. "They're basically designing the same thing: a rectangle. There's nothing more special about one [company's] rectangle than another's, except materials," Arieff says.

The problem is that simply making a prefab house isn't going to drive down costs or execution time. "Unless you do prefab at scale, you're never going to get any of the benefits that everyone gets so excited about," Arieff says. When I talked with cityLAB-UCLA's Dana Cuff, she shared similar concerns about companies that seemingly advertise a house you can click and buy. "You can't order up a house like that," she says. "You struggle with your site, the city planning department, assembling your subcontractors." All of these factors mean it takes time—years—to build just one unit. LA-Más's work is a prime example.

Also, Arieff notes that the companies getting into the space are appealing to the "*Dwell* prefab" style, referencing a certain luxury aesthetic. But this kind of home is unlikely to come cheap. "It's disingenuous to be saying that it will only cost $40,000," she says. Building an ADU in Arieff's hometown of San Francisco costs at minimum $500,000, she explains, when accounting for construction, engineering, and permitting, not to mention materials, appliances, and utility hookups. "When people say ADUs are going to solve the housing crisis—not at that entry point."

While Arieff acknowledges that many people could create a garage conversion or ADU on their property, the barrier to entry for most people is so high that it's not worth it. San Francisco averages about six hundred ADU permits issued per year. "To make even a dent in the city's housing crisis, cities need to streamline the process and maybe even consider subsidizing the costs," she says.

For Arieff, the solution has got to match the rhetoric. ADU manufacturers claiming to revolutionize housing have to be doing more than just selling variations on a rectangle. Multifamily housing has been more successful at harnessing prefab—or, more precisely, modular or manufactured housing. For those buildings, the inefficiencies of the permit process and site design can be offset by the cost savings of off-site construction for hundreds of units.

ONE ENTREPRENEUR WHO might actually meet Arieff's requirements is Steven Dietz. She'd probably roll her eyes at his thirty-two years as a venture-capital investor but warm up after hearing that he started his first business, United Dwelling, after feeling compelled to play some role in solving California's housing crisis. His company responds to the problems that Leung, Arieff, and others have been grappling with: affordability, scale, and timing.

There are an estimated four hundred thousand single-family homes with two-car garages in Los Angeles alone.[18] Recognizing that there are millions more around the country, Dietz found a typology that could scale. Most two-car garages have similar dimensions and site conditions. Many have extra space in them. What if they could house people?

Dietz also agreed with Leung and LA-Más that most people aren't equipped to become amateur developers. So, what if he created a company that converted garages into living spaces for homeowners? What if the homeowners didn't have to put in money up front to do this, but instead had to share their rental income with the company that took care of the garage conversion? There would be little risk of these ADUs ending up as inaccessibly expensive high-end housing. Even with nice materials and finishes, there is only so much one can charge to live in a converted garage.

United Dwelling solved the two biggest obstacles—time and money—and, as a result of its IKEA-like kit of parts, it could scale and be more affordable. It also got around the "fingerprint" problem that Dana Cuff mentioned. It took the downsides of the banal typology of single-family suburban homes and turned them into an advantage. There's little guesswork with a standard two-car garage. Even more exciting: it's potentially an open-source idea. United Dwelling can scale quickly because of the capital it has raised, but governments, nonprofit organizations, and school districts with their own financing could potentially copy this model to house, say, veterans, schoolteachers, artists, or other populations in need of inexpensive housing.

WHAT ARIEFF WANTS to see is a paradigm change in who is building and buying ADUs. She isn't excited by the shiny new start-ups but rather by the dowdy suburban builders who are getting into the game. She believes that changing the mainstream real estate industry is where ADUs and tiny homes will actually reach scale—not through individual property owners building their own units. When buyers of new homes are selecting finishes and styles, Arieff hopes one day developers ask, "Would you like a cathedral ceiling, walk-in closet, or an ADU?" Instead of retrofitting single-family lots to include an ADU, what if newly created housing had ADUs already built in?

Some forward-thinking builders like Lennar are already building models like this, and I'll discuss how they're particularly geared toward multigenerational families in the next chapter. Meanwhile, housing companies like Clayton Homes, the country's largest manufactured-housing developer, are getting into the tiny home business. Their "designer cottages" line offers a "low country" house or "saltbox," hinting at another trend here: accessing people's nostalgia for a simpler past, when a saltbox house wasn't tiny—just normal.

IN THE MEDIA, tiny homes have gotten attention as a kind of domestic cleanse, an opportunity to reset and rediscover what really matters, for people whose oversize homes have gotten in the way of their ability to live simply and spontaneously, or even to think creatively. Brent Heavener, author of *Tiny House: Live Small, Dream Big*, says, "Tiny houses are creative and strategic alternatives that keep you from falling into a societal trap and ending up like a lot of people around you."[19] Heavener's book looks at the beauty of living small, and it's this glorified vision that has gotten tiny homes all the attention. But the reality of much of the tiny-home industry is a far cry from dreaming big.

The Tiny House Festival, a roving convention that makes its way across the country every few weeks, adheres to the idea that tiny should be cheap and easy. I attended one of the festivals, held at the Florida State Fairgrounds near Tampa. The festival is taking place just feet away from a gun show and snake show. Here, tiny homes aren't compared to Teslas. Contextual design this is not.

The tiny-house models at the festival are typically about ten feet wide by twenty feet long. In those two hundred square feet, the homes feature a bed, kitchenette, and bathroom. On the outside, they emulate traditional cottages and Tudors. Inside are faux-brick walls and countertops that are made to look like marble but are actually laminate. Some are emulating that "*Dwell* prefab" style that Arieff mentioned—with boxy styling and spare, modern finishes—but most are trying to fit in as traditional suburban cottages. They have white trim and flourishes of decorative molding. The ADUs that Arieff and Cuff envision are bigger and of higher quality than the homes on display here; these are efficiencies in every sense of the word. Many feature lofted beds or pull-out futons. The bathrooms are so small your knees are under the sink if you sit on the toilet.

For all the talk of tiny homes being the new lifestyle choice, the reality is that many are traditional mobile homes in disguise. Most of them are set on gooseneck trailers that can be transported with a Ford F-150. Because mobile homes often carry so much stigma, tiny homes have replaced them in a move of brilliant marketing. I look around me at the couples carrying iced coffee, the single woman with a lapdog, the families with ebullient and curious children. People who would never think of living in a trailer home might be willing to accept living in a tiny home for a little while. Most of the festival is window-shopping for the home-curious. No one I speak to seems ready to buy a model off the floor, but rather they're here to see what all the fuss is about.

One of the vendors at the festival is Jill Kanto, a web developer and founder of Search Tiny House Villages, a website that helps tiny house owners find communities where they can park their homes. A few years ago, she found herself leaving her partner, and as a single mother with two kids, she needed cheap and stable housing that she had a measure of control over. She decided to build her own tiny home in Maryland, sited on a six-acre farm where she pays $500 per month for the privilege of keeping her home there. She then spent nearly $35,000 to build the house, where she says she misses none of the trappings of traditional living, other than the ability to comfortably host guests.

While the blog on Kanto's website has posts about the top three communities for dog lovers or near ski resorts, the reality of living in a tiny home isn't necessarily glamorous, nor was it meant to be. It reminds me of something that Ehrin Lingeman said when I asked her about the "lifestyle" of tiny homes. She responded matter-of-factly: "We live in someone's driveway, use their electricity, and get water from a garden hose." It's not an easy life, but it does come with dignity. The tiny-house lifestyle is in some sense a reimagination of the pioneering spirit that originally attracted many people to rural and small-town living. Many in tiny homes pride themselves on doing more with less, on living lightly on the land and within their means. Most of all, they feel like they have freedom. High rent can be oppressive and anxiety inducing, and getting out from under it can be liberating. Likewise, the tight confines of a tiny home mean strictly avoiding accumulating possessions. For those who can't afford to buy extra stuff, a tiny home usefully doesn't allow for unnecessary objects.

These are the same talking points made over and over again among the vendors at the Tiny House Festival. By having less space, less stuff, and less financial stress, a weight has been lifted. It's a counterpoint to Americans' typically insatiable consumerism and the way that many equate stuff with happiness.

All of the tiny-home dwellers I speak to have been required to do some DIY problem-solving to figure out how to live within a tiny home, but rather than this being a drawback—something that the people in luxury co-living buildings, for example, would happily outsource—they find this kind of work empowering. For Lingeman, it was dealing with that garden-hose water line when it freezes over in the winter; for Kanto, it was learning how to insulate a home and sharing her knowledge with others.

Will they live tiny forever? Kanto says the answer is yes. Lingeman would prefer to live in a more modestly sized house if she could afford one. Even so, her perspective on homes, what goes in them, and how she could use space has permanently changed. Now when she sees large houses, she no longer pines for one. Instead she thinks, "I could never even imagine what I could put in those houses."

AS I WALKED around the festival, I couldn't help but notice one home unlike all the others. Unlike the cute cottages and sleek modernist bungalows, this home was a stark, twenty-foot shipping container with no attempt at curb appeal. Inside was Glen Gibellina, a white-haired retired contractor turned activist living in Manatee County, Florida. While all the other tiny homes on display were mass-produced models trucked in for the event, Gibellina and a handful of high school students had built his prototype. Gibellina wasn't exactly looking to make a sale (although that would have been nice). Instead, he was there to talk about tiny homes as a solution to the affordable housing crisis.

Becoming a housing advocate wasn't part of Gibellina's plan. His first shipping-container house was built for the practical purpose of having a guesthouse that he could use as an Airbnb. But when he heard that there were an estimated eight hundred homeless students in his county, and that many of the area teachers couldn't afford to live near the school because of housing costs, he quickly thought to put his experience to work for the benefit of his community.

Gibellina found that you could take a twenty-foot shipping container, fix it up with off-the-shelf materials from Home Depot and basic furniture from IKEA, and make a decent home. He also realized that he could teach high school and community college students not only how to physically construct a building, but how to think differently about building housing in their community. He partnered with CareerSource Florida, which he says is going to pay for former inmates trained in welding to work for him.

Manatee County sits just north of Sarasota. With about four hundred thousand people, the county isn't Florida's biggest or wealthiest area, but it is, like much of the country, struggling with affordability issues. What makes Florida unique is its relatively lax laws governing ADUs.

So Gibellina started a company, Uncontained360, and recruited dozens of students from the local Bayshore High School to build a prototype tiny home from a twenty-foot-by-eight-foot container. Gibellina and the students put together a very modest 160-square-foot home with a pull-out futon, kitchen, and bathroom. Gibellina's goal is to find homeowners willing to buy or even borrow these tiny homes and put them in their backyard, renting to students or teachers who are living in nightly motels, shelters, or a car.

Not everyone has the time or money that Gibellina has to build and install shipping-container homes. Not every city has lax enough zoning or licenses and inspections departments to pull this off. But Gibellina's work illustrates the desperate search for inexpensive, fast, and replicable ways to house the homeless and housing insecure.

THE PROCESS OF adding ADUs to single-family homes runs counter to the fundamental way that people have created housing for the past century. A zoning code that gives homeowners the option of adding to or subdividing their home to create an additional housing unit is a phenomenal shift in the relationship between people, property, and government. Whether it is a custom-built house, a prefab rectangle bought online, a tiny house on a trailer, or a converted garage, accessory dwelling units are the opposite of the American dream—they're the American way of making do.

The lessons of ADUs should also extend beyond the geographies of suburban settings. In the New York City area, the Regional Plan Association published a plan in 2018 that calls out ADUs as something that zoning should explicitly allow for:

> Zoning should be reformed such that every single-family dwelling is allowed a second dwelling unit if it meets appropriate

fire and building codes. Other accessory dwelling units should be allowed by reforming rules related to light, air, relation to ground level, and other laws and regulations that do not affect safety, while retaining strict safety and housing quality measures appropriate for modern life. Approximately 100,000 new homes could be added in New York City alone by instituting these reforms, and potentially up to 300,000 throughout the region.[20]

To boot, allowing ADUs would increase the city's property-tax revenue and more than offset the costs of added regulation.

In September 2019, California passed legislation allowing two ADUs to be built on properties zoned for single-family homes. It competes with Washington State—which passed legislation that would permit two ADUs per property, cap fees on new construction, and allow flexible design requirements— for the most far-reaching pro-ADU legislation in the country.

These new laws only add to the evidence that cultural shifts are creating a climate where small homes can't be blocked much longer. New design ideas and technologies that cleverly take advantage of small quarters and a more urgent need for affordability have made it impossible to ignore the tiny trend. Local and state policymakers who reverse regulations that have prevented new production of small homes find that they have unleashed tremendous interest in this type of housing.

Banks are also recognizing the growing importance of small and accessory homes, sensing new financing opportunities. Tiny homes—because of both their size and their portability—often don't qualify for typical loans. But banks and nontraditional lenders like CDFIs are looking into the potential for a nonpredatory refinancing scheme where people can leverage their main house to build an accessory dwelling. Meanwhile, the rise of ADUs is dramatically changing the math of homeownership. Homeowners are seeking mortgage relief at the same time that tenants are looking for affordable housing. Many Americans have borrowed against their houses to keep up with the rising cost of life—such as college tuition or buying a car—and need a new form of income. When talking about the explosive interest in ADUs, Cuff says there hasn't been so much housing production in California since World War II, a time when the mortgage industry was reshaped as well. Hopefully the resounding interest in ADUs will mean new creative financial products that will enable a larger segment of the country to construct them.

With growing acceptance of tiny houses and ADUs come implications for how we think about family. ADUs can allow extended families to live closer with a greater degree of privacy and personal space. Cuff notes that there is always a story behind why people want an ADU. While there are many Section 8 tenants, students, and others who need this type of housing, Cuff says many of the stories she hears are about women and caregiving: women who are either caring for children who aren't yet ready to be on their own or for parents who need help. It's somewhat surprising that it has taken so long for housing to catch up with this kind of need, given that generations have always had to look after each other. Cuff believes there's so much more to be done to make life better for families, a goal that she recognizes takes time. "This will continue to occupy my professional life indefinitely," Cuff says.

CHAPTER SIX

DIFFERENT GENERATIONS, ONE ROOF

T HE CHICAGO TWO-FLAT IS the city's answer to the Brooklyn brownstone and the Philadelphia row house. Built at the turn of the twentieth century by and for European immigrants, the two-flat was a type of two-story housing intended as a compromise between a single-family home and living with boarders. With a two-flat, owners got the best of both worlds: a family could live in one unit and rent out the other for income, while still maintaining privacy. A century before people went crazy over accessory dwelling units, two-flats had them built in.

The style of home proliferated throughout the city, such that two- to four-flat buildings now make up more than a quarter of Cook County's total housing stock and one-third of its rentals. And that's even with Chicago's gentrification encouraging numerous developers and homeowners to convert two-flats into single-family homes.[1]

When Mike Healy was looking for a way to afford a home with his wife, a two-flat was an obvious way to do it. He was highly wary of buying a home after having seen what his parents had gone through. His parents were both attorneys whose health deteriorated earlier than anticipated, in their fifties and sixties. Their decline and the housing downturn coincided, and he saw how all their liquidity was wrapped up in their home, which they couldn't sell. "It was the collocation of the single most inelastic commodity, life savings, and net worth," he recalls.

He watched as they struggled to maintain their home while suffering from illness and early onset dementia. "The house was the Gordian knot against which all loose ends of their life became unmanageable, and they developed unhealthy coping strategies to deal with it," he says. Located in a strictly residential area, the house made access to amenities all but impossible as their conditions deteriorated. When the housing market went into free fall, it knocked out what wealth they had accumulated, making it hard for them to afford assisted living. The situation—isolated and immobile—accelerated their decline, in Healy's opinion.

Healy came away from the experience with a new perspective on how he wanted to live. "I would rather rent and pay whatever premium rather than colocate my financial well-being with an inelastic commodity." So Healy and his wife found a two-flat in Logan Square and rented from two brothers who had moved to the exurbs over an hour away. The landlords charged below-market rent in exchange for tenants who never called or asked them to fix anything. Healy then subleased the upstairs apartment to his sister and her boyfriend for a while.

But when Healy's sister moved out, he, like so many Americans, felt pressure to get a foothold in the local housing market.

If he and his wife didn't buy a home in the next few years, he wondered if they'd ever be able to. Two-flats in the neighborhood were often called "deconversion candidates," which could be turned into single-family homes for $900,000. As a hedge against getting priced out of the neighborhood, Healy and his wife then bought the house from their landlords.

Around the same time, they began to notice that Healy's mother-in-law was getting older and had fewer ties where she lived in California. She was living by herself and entering her sixties, the phase of life when social isolation can begin to set in. Healy wanted to avoid his mother-in-law having the same problems his own parents had had. He wondered what they would do if his mother-in-law got sick. At this point, Healy and his wife were raising two young children. The prospect of his wife flying to take care of her mother every few weeks was unappealing on so many levels. But the more important question was, Why wait until his mother-in-law got sick to be involved in her care or spend time with her? Why not, this time around, try to prevent the kind of care crisis his own parents experienced?

Once again, the two-flat came in handy. Healy could offer his mother-in-law the chance to live with her daughter and her grandchildren, but with a good deal of privacy. Healy's mother-in-law could have the upstairs apartment to herself and come downstairs to a welcoming family when she wanted.

It did not take much convincing to get Healy's mother-in-law to move to Chicago. She could spend more time with her grandchildren, help out by babysitting, and also share meals with her daughter and Healy. Whereas before she was living alone and checking in occasionally by phone, "Now she feels vitally necessary and useful," Healy says.

Healy and his wife refinanced the home, adding his mother-in-law as a deed holder and getting some cash to pay for a basement renovation. Having a third adult paying for the house's upkeep and mortgage has created a little bit of an economic surplus. Healy also sees a "social-familial surplus" in having a third adult in the house. While his mother-in-law is not directly responsible for her grandkids, she has the authority that a grandparent conveys. She keeps an open-door policy with the kids, so they can run upstairs whenever they want to see their grandmother—for a little attention or a change of scenery. Inevitably the generations of the family see each other every day, but the adults navigate privacy a little differently. There are motion-sensor lights in the stairwell that separates their apartments, giving a few seconds' warning if someone is coming up or down the stairs for a visit. It's a good metaphor for their approach to living together: while they share four walls, they're conscientious that they have private space, and it's important to be aware of the cues indicating when company is welcome or not. "Yesterday's favor can be tomorrow's expectation," Healy says, noting that just because he makes dinner for everyone one night or his mother-in-law offers to get the groceries one day, it doesn't mean that these one-off gestures should become obligations.

That said, there is an abundance of favors from Healy's mother-in-law. Healy sounds downright gleeful discussing how she will always take the baby monitor after the kids are in bed, allowing Healy and his wife a chance to go out almost any night without having to pay for a babysitter or worry they need to book childcare in advance. "She'll keep the monitor and save the kids if the house burns down," he says with a laugh.

But the main advantage for Healy is knowing how his mother-in-law is doing. Without proximity to his own parents,

Healy may have missed warning signs that their health was at risk. In seeing his mother-in-law every day, Healy knows that she is being taken care of and is ensuring her own best health and independence. He calls this approach "offense to play defense," and it's a way of thinking about aging and illness that few families consider, even though it's a strategy increasingly used by employers and governments to rein in health-care costs and improve people's wellness. By checking in on the health of people more frequently, these institutions can get early warning signs if something is headed in the wrong direction and more easily change course.

Although living in a multigenerational household hasn't been proven to improve outcomes for people already dealing with an illness, it has been shown to help healthy people live longer lives.[2] While living with extended family can be stressful for some, for others—particularly those who voluntarily live with an extra generation—it can be a boon. Healy's example hits on many of the advantages of multigenerational households: less social isolation for grandparents, more care for young children, childcare flexibility, and economic savings, to name a few. These are some of the biggest issues facing young families, aging baby boomers, and anyone struggling to make rent today. What if multigenerational housing was, in fact, a key to solving so many of the problems confronting our country? What if it offered a way to live in a better house at a lower cost, a way to enable a better life for families, and a way to stay healthy and connected in a time when most housing discourages it?

MULTIGENERATIONAL LIVING—DEFINED BY the Census Bureau as three generations or more living under the same roof—is on the rise throughout the United States, reaching its highest levels since 1950. A number of factors account for the rise: an aging population, high housing costs, an increasing number of Hispanic and Asian households (which have a tradition and propensity to live multigenerationally), and delayed independence among twentysomethings.[3] As of 2018, sixty-four million Americans lived multigenerationally, or more than 20 percent of the population.[4] Not only are people increasingly living with their parents and children, but with kin—sisters and brothers, aunts and uncles. In 2018, the average American household size ticked up for the first time since 1850, in part due to extended families living together.[5] With all the demographic trends behind multigenerational living projected to continue into the near future, there's no reason to think this style will reverse. Still, housing that purposefully accommodates multigenerational living is rare.

As we've seen in the previous chapters, various forms of shared living were common until the postwar era, and then became less popular as many municipalities adopted restrictive zoning codes. But unlike those housing types, multigenerational housing was never explicitly outlawed or targeted by exclusive zoning. It simply fell out of style, first gradually in the late nineteenth and early twentieth century, then rapidly in the second half of the twentieth century. As economic conditions changed the advantages and disadvantages of families living together—and as the invention of the American Dream of getting one's own home discouraged multigenerational living—fewer and fewer families had the financial or social incentives to live this way.

But in the middle of the nineteenth century, multigenerational housing was almost universal among the elderly. Since families tended to be large, not all children lived with their parents, but almost all parents lived with one of their children.[6] Multigenerational living wasn't always—or even often—a life-long style of living, but rather the short phase when grand-parents were old and the youngest generation was young. Steven Ruggles, a professor of history and population studies at the University of Minnesota, describes how omnipresent mul-tigenerational living was during this time:

> In the mid-nineteenth century, about 70 per cent of persons aged 65 or older lived with their children or children-in-law. In addition, about a tenth of the elderly lived with other relatives—mainly grandchildren, siblings, nephews, and nieces. Another tenth lived with non-relatives; most of these were boarders, but some were household heads who kept boarders or servants. Only 11 percent of the elderly in 1850 lived alone or with only their spouses, and only 0.7 percent lived in insti-tutions such as almshouses and homes for the aged.[7]

While many today think of multigenerational households as less economically secure, in the nineteenth and early twen-tieth centuries the poor were less likely to be in a multigenera-tional household. Additional household members added to the financial resources and stability of the family, but also wealthier families were more incentivized to keep their descendants close by. Families who lived multigenerationally not only accumu-lated wealth together, but were well positioned to pass on their wealth and property. Interestingly, economic and geographic mobility were at their highest when rates of intergenerational living were too, suggesting that multigenerational living didn't historically hinder people's ability to take advantage of new professional or personal opportunities.[8]

But if multigenerational living was so beneficial, why did it fall out of favor? As Ruggles notes, it was deeply tied to a lifestyle centered around the family farm. These farms depended on family members to work the land, and allowed older family members to age in place with financial security. When America's agricultural economy gave way to wage labor, often located in cities or in company towns, the family farm that tied generations together fell out of favor. Younger family members were no longer incentivized to stay on the farm. As younger generations sought the greater fortune and opportunity that came with modern, industrial businesses, the farm was no longer a prized inheritance.[9] As more young people found success leaving their family behind, moving out of the family home became equated with success.

In 1935, Social Security was established. While the income that elders brought in could be seen as an added resource for a multigenerational family, some studies have shown that it enabled and supported independent seniors, particularly in the second half of the twentieth century.[10] Now that the elderly could move out of their children's homes if they chose—and now that children felt less obligation to take their parents in—multigenerational living lost yet another advantage. At the same time, family size continued to decrease, and with fewer children there was not always a child who could support his or her parents as they aged.

Another significant cause of shifting lifestyles was suburbanization and the expansion of less expensive housing options. As housing costs went down in the middle of the twentieth century, families and elders could afford to live separately. By 1980, just 12 percent of American households lived multigenerationally.[11]

But rather than continue to decline from there, multigenerational housing has risen in popularity again. The 1980s saw a host of legislation that scaled back welfare, including the Aid to Families with Dependent Children program (the predecessor to Temporary Assistance for Needy Families, or TANF). As families saw their access to benefits decline, they moved in together to save money and pool resources. Housing costs also began to escalate in cities after bottoming out in many places in the early 1970s.[12] At the same time, immigration patterns changed. The country's immigrant population was just 4.7 percent (9.6 million) in 1970. That number has steadily risen, and was up to 13.4 percent of the country's total population in 2015.[13] All of these economic and social factors have contributed to a rise in families living together out of necessity or tradition.

At the same time, gender roles have shifted. More women are going to work: In 1950, women accounted for just one-third of the total workforce.[14] Nowadays, they make up roughly 47 percent.[15] Additionally, many women have become either the primary breadwinner of the family, despite their partner's participation in the workforce, or the head of the household as a single mother. Multigenerational living has become more appealing, as live-in grandparents can provide childcare or other domestic support and enable more women to work full-time jobs. Nearly one in ten American children live in multigenerational households.[16]

Today, more people are in a multigenerational living situation than ever before—while the percentage is the same as it was in 1950, the actual number of people has doubled (sixty-four million today versus thirty-two million back then).[17] For many, it's a simple economic proposition: living with family provides an opportunity to share expenses and possibly live in better housing than each generation could separately. Student loans and other kinds of debt have made independent living impossible for many young people, while the 2008 recession made independent retirement more difficult for seniors. It's not a coincidence that the steepest rise in multigenerational living occurred from 2009 to 2014, when an extra 9.1 million people moved in with family at a time when the country was slowly emerging from recession.[18] Depending on how long it takes for the economy to recover from the COVID-19 pandemic, the country may see yet more increases in multigenerational living.

For others, living with extended family is a way of coping with the time and money required to raise children these days. Formal day care has become incredibly expensive—the average cost of day care programs was just under $1,000 per month in a 2015 study and can be much more expensive in high-cost cities.[19] This means that the cost of childcare has increased by 2,000 percent in the past forty years.[20] Mothers who want to work but can't afford day care are often housebound, unless they find a family member willing to pitch in and look after their children for free. Other women aren't comfortable with formal day care or may need childcare outside the typical nine-to-five, and prefer to have family members look after their children. Multigenerational housing can help working women make ends meet and support their schedule.

Finally, baby boomers, the more than seventy million Americans who make up the country's second-largest demographic cohort, are now in their retirement years. For those who are not tied to their communities by work, who may not have the income to support an independent lifestyle and aren't interested in a retirement community, multigenerational housing might be a perfect fit. Additionally, while widowed grandparents were always prime candidates for an in-law suite, the rising divorce rate for seniors is creating a new set of parents who are eager to move in with their adult children.

While these scenarios frame multigenerational housing as a form of coping with hardship, there are many families for whom it is traditional to live together. As of 2018, 29 percent of Asian families, 27 percent of Hispanic families, and 26 percent of black families live multigenerationally, compared with just 15 percent of white families.[21] The National Institutes of Health noted that foreign-born populations accustomed to multigenerational living may find the interpersonal dynamics of family-centered living situations less stressful than native-born populations in the United States do, and that three-generation households have more social capital or helpful networks than single-generation households.[22] In many non-Western cultures, families believe in a kind of filial piety, or respecting and taking care of one's elders. As a result, living with grandparents is seen less as a burden than as an important responsibility.

The research fails to show a statistical health benefit for all multigenerational households, perhaps because of confounding factors—for one, those living together out of necessity rather than by choice may also be under stress. But the data do suggest that multigenerational living could be a social and economic boost for those who are willingly living this way.[23]

Other countries feel so strongly about supporting multigenerational housing, or intergenerational communities, that they put monetary incentives behind it. In Singapore, for example, the government will pay you to live with or near your elderly relatives. Singapore's Proximity Housing Grant program pays families 30,000 Singapore dollars (or about $21,500) to move within two kilometers (or about 1.25 miles) of grandparents or children in one of the government's Housing and Development Board homes.[24] In Hong Kong, the government prioritizes applications from multigenerational families that live together or near each other for access to senior-oriented public housing.[25]

Countries where the government pays for health care are eager to find a way to reduce hospital visits and health-care costs for the elderly. Having live-in or nearby support is clearly one way to achieve that goal. Germany has looked at the psychological side effects and isolation of aging, and has supported the construction of 540 *Mehrgenerationenhäuser*, or intergenerational communities.[26] These centers, which often serve as a kind of day care for both the young and old, enable interaction between seniors and children in the hopes of giving seniors opportunities to contribute to and engage with the next generation.

Rather than encouraging multigenerational households, the United States essentially discourages them. Multifamily properties, like Mike Healy's two-flat, are more difficult to finance than single-family homes. When Healy initially sought to purchase his home, the combination of the fact that it was a multifamily home and that it was within three hundred feet of a gas station made it a nonstarter for an FHA government loan. He and his wife instead had to cobble together money from personal loans to pay for the house. Multifamily homes are essentially considered commercial properties, and as such are ineligible for standard FHA mortgages. As a result, a swath of buyers who would benefit from FHA's low down-payment requirements and low rates are discouraged from purchasing these properties.

Government benefit programs can also effectively discourage co-residence among low-income families. People applying for Supplemental Security Income (SSI) from Social Security can be discouraged from living with family, since having access to "free food and shelter" can count as income—and the more income, the lower the SSI benefits. Similarly, Supplemental Nutrition Assistance Program (SNAP) benefits are dependent on the total income of a household. So, while you do get more SNAP benefits if a member of the household is over sixty, you are penalized if the combined household income is over the SNAP threshold. The monthly income limit for SNAP benefits for a two-person household is $1,832 in Pennsylvania in 2020; each extra person adds just $479 per month toward the income limit. So a single mother and child could get SNAP if the mother's total income is less than approximately $21,984 per year; meanwhile, if that mother and child move in with two grandparents, the household's total income can be no more than approximately $39,228 if they want to receive SNAP benefits. Unlike other countries that see the upside of extended families living together, our government provides no incentives for multigenerational living, and instead has programs with a bias against larger households pooling resources.

But it's not just the government that has been slow to acknowledge its bias. The media routinely denigrates multigenerational living. When a family lives with another adult, it's called "doubling up." Children who leave home for college and return are called "boomerang" kids or said to be "failing to launch." In general, situations outside the norms of living as a nuclear family, a couple, or alone are met with hand-wringing: How will young people who live with their parents forge their own independence, partner up, and build wealth? Is our economy failing if twentysomethings or young families can't live on their own? Multigenerational housing makes the media uncomfortable, as it runs counter to the model of self-sufficiency that has long underpinned the homeownership lifestyle and the American Dream.

Yet, despite these deterrents, multigenerational living continues to gain in popularity. Can a niche part of the housing industry become a bigger part of the mainstream? Could new policies or programs help more people benefit from a style of living that is too often inaccessible? What will it take for companies and entrepreneurs to create products geared toward this market of sixty-four million people?

JANE MARIE O'CONNOR has been studying the housing industry for twenty-five years, beginning with a role as a publisher of guides to senior living in seven states. Through the course of her work, she became well connected with senior-living administrators and occupants. She developed a deep knowledge about senior-living options: communities for active lifestyles with no services, residences with tons of amenities, retirement communities, independent-living apartments, assisted living—the list goes on.

With her industry knowledge, she went on to consult for builders, developers, and organizations like the National Association of Home Builders in the United States and around the world. But despite her focus on housing for people over the age of fifty-five, O'Connor has seen little innovation in multigenerational housing. "We have more blended families than ever, more grandparents taking care of grandchildren—whether because of the opioid epidemic, the high divorce rate, lack of employment opportunities, or an inability to fulfill parental responsibilities," she says. Yet, there are few communities that are intentionally supporting both people over fifty-five and kids under eighteen with a mix of amenities and housing types that benefit all.

Part of the reason for this disconnect is something called the Housing for Older Persons Act (HOPA), passed in 1995, which amended the anti-discriminatory Fair Housing Act to enable developers to market and sell units in communities specifically created for a fifty-five-plus demographic. But part of the law states that no one under nineteen may live in these communities, and that 80 percent of the housing stock must be reserved for those over fifty-five. "These neighborhood settings would be wonderful for children, with security and a sense of belonging. However, they exclude those grandchildren. They're not geared toward them," O'Connor says. A 2011 study from MetLife and the NAHB found that nearly one-third of people over the age of fifty-five live in communities that entirely or mostly comprise people of the same age group.

Few of these communities are geared toward anyone seeking an affordable home. The senior-living industry came into its own in the 1990s and early 2000s, when homeownership was peaking and prices in many places were too. As a way to distinguish new senior housing from the standards of senior living at the time—nursing homes that many seniors feared, or faith-related communities that weren't as inclusive or geared toward active retirement as some might like—many of these developments were aimed at a high-end market rather than an affordability-driven one. Few at the time anticipated that, in the future, there would be so many seniors raising their grandchildren or housing their own children for a spell.

The success of fifty-five-plus communities hints at a pathway for building more multigenerational housing. With the help of the HOPA law, a whole subset of real estate was created and an industry built up around it. Could something similar materialize to support multigenerational families? Could entire communities be dedicated to them, with housing specifically designed for their needs?

Some major housing developers, like Lennar and Pardee Homes, have created new housing models that intentionally incorporate a "multigenerational unit" or "estate suite." Lennar's Next Gen model is billed as "the home within a home." With the entire house located on one level, the Next Gen has a separate suite with bedroom, bathroom, kitchenette, small living space, and garage. Multigenerational gated communities can be found in California and Arizona, with high prices reflective of their exclusivity. But few developers have opted to create multigenerational communities at a price point that has mass appeal. Why?

The market for multigenerational housing is less white and less wealthy than for other housing types. Housing markets haven't historically been kind to low-income and minority buyers. At a time when the president of the United States has put forward an array of anti-immigrant policies, it's unlikely we'll see new developments or policies that intentionally accommodate families with non-US-born members who live outside the norm of a single, nuclear family.

Housing developers and cities might have other reasons for not encouraging multigenerational housing. After all, it could discourage or delay young people's first home purchase, and it also cuts back on the amount of furniture and appliances that each person needs to buy. In general, it's out of sync with traditional capitalist models and it might add density that communities have traditionally tried to avoid. But multigenerational living has demographics on its side—it's only going to get more common. Wouldn't it make sense for cities and developers to find a way to harness the popularity of this trend?

SIMILAR TO MULTIGENERATIONAL families, there is an increasing trend of grandfamilies, where grandparents are the primary caregivers for children. There are about two dozen housing projects around the country that are custom-built for grandparents who are raising their grandchildren. Las Abuelitas, a modest complex of twelve homes organized around a central courtyard and community center in South Tucson, is one of the best. South Tucson is a tiny municipality: just 1.2 square miles with a little over 5,600 people. Most of those people are poor: 50 percent of its population lives in poverty, making it Arizona's poorest city. But it is also vibrant, with plenty of Mexican restaurants and stores, and enough trendy cafés nearby to make people nervous about gentrification and displacement.

According to Generations United, some 7.8 million children live with grandparents or close relatives other than their parents, and 2.5 million grandparents report being the primary caregiver for their grandchildren.[27] Coalitions of grandparent caregivers are trying to encourage housing that speaks to their unique needs and helps build community among their families. In Tucson, a group of grandparents associated with Kinship and Adoption Resource and Education (KARE) urged a local nonprofit, the Primavera Foundation, to build a community for grandfamilies. Primavera is a decades-old Tucson organization with the mission of "providing pathways out of poverty."

It runs a host of housing programs, from emergency housing and homeless shelters, to affordable rental housing, to home-ownership and financial education programs. It was the perfect partner to bring Las Abuelitas to life, because it was able to address the needs of grandfamilies and low-income families at the same time.

As you enter the Las Abuelitas courtyard, you stand among a dozen raised beds of kale and broccoli; fruit trees bearing or-anges, figs, and guavas; a few bike racks; and a basketball hoop on a multipurpose play space. A solar array doubles as a shading element over some benches; it has also enabled Las Abuelitas to be LEED Platinum and helps keep household utility bills to about $20 per month. Your average low-income housing, this is not.

Elementary school kids let themselves in through this courtyard and into a community space where an after-school program is getting under way. Two instructors teach a game in the main room, but the space also has a community kitchen, a reading room, and a computer lab. While not one of the city-run rec centers, the courtyard and the community space are open to anyone and essentially function as a civic commons. About half the kids going to the class are from Las Abuelitas, the others from nearby public housing and private homes.

Through a gate with a keypad, open only to residents, is where the two-bedroom homes are located, along with a small grassy area with boulders for kids to climb. Another half acre or so pro-vides trees, grass, and a place for dogs to run. It's clear that these are spaces for learning and playing, and though there's no one using the outdoors on the brisk January day when I visited, I can imagine how different generations enjoy the spaces for activity or respite. Peggy Hutchison, Primavera's executive director, gives me a tour, noting the lack of green space in the rest of South Tucson. For many kids, this may be their only exposure to it.

Hutchison specializes in this kind of matching between what her organization can provide and what is lacking in her city. When Primavera began work on the project in 2012, Hutchison found there were some 8,500 grandparents raising children in the area. Many of the children were coping with fractured families. Some may have had a parent return to Latin America (the Mexican border is just sixty miles away); others may have had a parent in prison. Whatever the reason, this group wanted housing that would better support their community.

The grandparents wanted houses where kids could play outside with other kids but not roam too far. A kitchen that was open to dining and living space was essential, so they could keep an eye on the children while cooking a meal. Each house has its own patio, with shutters that can be opened to the common areas of the complex or closed for privacy. These small design decisions make a difference in how families enjoy the balance between private and public space. Hutchison recalls it was important to the grandparents to have two bathrooms in a two-bedroom unit. For some grandparents, that second bathroom was their only private, calm space.

Las Abuelitas is a haven for kids being raised by kin—not only by grandmas, as the name of the community suggests, but also by uncles, older sisters, and single parents. Las Abuelitas is actually unable to directly market its housing to grandfamilies because it was built on HUD-owned property and is bound by fair-housing laws intended to prevent discrimination. It does restrict its tenants to households below 80 percent of the area median income threshold. Whoever lives there, Las Abuelitas is focused on "people, place, and community."

Las Abuelitas is just one of Primavera's developments that goes beyond the single-family home. They have renovated buildings into SROs for singles and couples who need affordable housing. Hutchison recalls her grandmother, who lived in a rooming house in Palo Alto, and how different styles of housing once existed in cities. Tucson is sprawling, with acre-wide parking lots, but she says the housing crisis is becoming a problem. "Yes, it's reached Tucson," she says.

THE IRONY OF the American housing crisis is that much of American housing is actually under-occupied. According to studies, there are somewhere between forty and sixty-five million spare bedrooms in existing housing stock. While companies like Airbnb have staked their business around this data point, multigenerational housing could use it too.

Nesterly is a start-up that helps seniors who have empty bedrooms find young tenants in need of less-expensive housing. Marketed as "homeshare with another generation," Nesterly provides a transactional framework for the oftentimes squishy work of connecting old and young people for mutual benefit.

Many of the advantages that come with home-sharing are the same as with multigenerational living within a family: greater economy, more human interaction, and more support for both parties. Nesterly helps codify the exchange: hosts can choose ways to lower the rent by having tenants pitch in on housework. A host can propose, for instance, eight hours per month of yard work or pet-care help for a $50 reduction on the rent.

The idea for Nesterly came to founder Noelle Marcus because she had extensive experience with intergenerational friendships. Marcus grew up on an island in British Columbia the size of Manhattan, but with just one thousand people on it. It takes three ferries and eight hours to get there from Vancouver. "It was so small that if you didn't become friends with the three other people your age, you had to become friends with people older or younger than you," Marcus says. As a result, many of her closest friends are still from her hometown, but they're also significantly different ages (she is thirty-five). "It's something I realize made me stand out among my friends and peers, this ability to connect to people in other ages. That's what a small community requires of you. Any community event or social event always had people of different generations. It was such a small place and everyone was included."

Spending time with other people's families and with people of different ages was a continuous theme throughout her life. When she traveled in high school to Australia or in college to Europe, or when she lived in New York as a student, she lived in homestays, home-shares, or with family friends. Relating to people from different generations has always seemed natural to her. One of her best friends is her grandmother, who is turning ninety and lives in New York. "She's my grandmother but also feels like a peer, like my friend," she says.

These personal experiences then informed her professional work in economic development and affordable housing. She worked at the New York City Economic Development Corporation on an $8.2 billion affordable housing plan—a great introduction to housing policy and finance. Then she went to MIT, where she studied urban planning with a focus on housing. Swirling around her studies and her personal life were these issues of affordable housing and intergenerational connection.

Oh, and data too: those millions of spare bedrooms in the country seemed like a problem, given the housing crunch in places like Boston. "I worked backwards into the solution," she says of the eureka moment that started Nesterly. She developed the business in her last semester at MIT in the spring of 2017, not only to match renters with bedrooms, but to match people across ages. Her background gave her the conviction that it was just as important to provide a service that would foster friendship and guard against social isolation as it was to help people find housemates. "This kind of human connection can be really powerful. We're inherently designed to do this and live this way."

She signed a contract with the City of Boston's Housing Innovation Lab just two weeks after graduating. Boston had recently created an Age-Friendly Boston Action Plan, as seniors were noted as the fastest-growing demographic in the city, and Nesterly fit squarely within the goals of that program. At the same time, a Trulia study showed that Boston's baby boomers had thirty-four thousand spare bedrooms available, and that graduate students could save $24,000 per year by renting a room in a house with another resident rather than a private one-bedroom.

Rather than start Nesterly off with an app or website, Marcus's process was more iterative. She spent more than six months matching just sixteen people through simple systems like Google Forms. The process was labor intensive, but at the end of it, she had learned a lot about who her potential customers would be and what they wanted. Surprisingly, it was the younger people who responded emotionally to the idea. She recalls the story of a graduate student who had never eaten his meals alone and was grappling with social isolation in a city where he knew no one. "Loneliness isn't just facing one generation. It's an issue that's affecting all of us," Marcus says.

Age segregation was another issue she ran into. While there's lots of conversation about race and class segregation, "people don't talk about the age aspect as much," Marcus says. Studies have shown that seniors rarely talk to young people about "important matters" like politics and the state of the world.[28] Marcus thinks Nesterly has the potential to help bridge some of the divides in politics and worldviews by simply encouraging generations to talk and listen to one another. "I've just drunk my own Kool-Aid," she jokes.

On a more practical level, she found that the platform didn't resonate as much with the very elderly (who are perhaps accustomed to living alone), but with people who had recently become empty nesters and were jarred by the experience of not having their kids around. Those empty nesters still had spare bedrooms in good shape, but they also had bills for their kids in college. Nesterly could bring hosts income while helping them through the emotional transition of living without kids. As a result, Nesterly's average host age is sixty-six.

As of the fall of 2019, Nesterly had booked more than thirty thousand nights through its service, helped a couple of hundred people find housemates, and secured housing for young people that is 30 to 60 percent less expensive than renting a standalone apartment. Marcus has also received interest from municipalities and individuals all over the world who think that Nesterly would be perfect for their community. Many of them are looking to activate their senior populations, help younger people find affordable housing, and in general address the empty-bedroom problem that makes their city's housing less efficient than it could be. "There's just such a need," Marcus says. "And there aren't enough options at an affordable price point."

Boston is just the beginning. "We want to bring this solution to other cities dealing with rapidly aging populations, an affordable housing crisis, and issues of social isolation," she says. Nesterly launched in Columbus, Ohio, in fall 2019 and is planning to launch in Louisville, Kentucky, in 2020. In the next five years, Marcus hopes that Nesterly will be in every high-cost city in North America and potentially around the world. The challenge then becomes scaling the business in such a way that it is still responsive to local communities.

Local organizations aren't the only ones clamoring for this. Marcus has found that Medicare Advantage providers are interested in Nesterly. As we'll see in the next chapter, many companies and governments are interested in housing that can reduce health-care costs.

HOW DOES MULTIGENERATIONAL housing play out for the vast majority of people who don't live in a two-flat or participate in a new app like Nesterly? It might look like Shinta Johnson's living situation. She and her husband live in the Germantown section of Philadelphia with two of their children, their spouses, and two grandchildren under one year old. Johnson, a retiree, is happy that her three-story, five-bedroom house, with two full baths and two half baths, can accommodate her kids at this critical moment. "It keeps them closer to me," she says. She loves that her grandchildren can grow up together for a period of time.

Johnson sees multigenerational living as a way to help her children out, hopefully so that they can save up enough money to buy houses of their own. But, she adds, "I don't ever want them to get too comfortable with being here."

At Johnson's, "everybody goes to work, everybody takes care of their own." In this way, her household is like a small cooperative. She doesn't set a standardized rent. Instead, everyone helps to keep the house running. "The kids know there are bills to be paid and give something once or twice a month," she says. That said, there are a few rules: most critically, keep the kitchen clean.

Right now, the plan is to have everyone live there for another year or so. But if the house were better designed for multigenerational living, she would consider encouraging her kids to stay longer. "If there were multiple kitchens, we'd be good, we could all live here together," she says.

Johnson's situation epitomizes the current predicament for many young families. Lots of new parents move back in with relatives to get some help with childcare and save money on housing to afford new costs like diapers, formula, kids' clothes, and toys. But while Johnson has space to host everyone, her house isn't specially designed for extended family. It's for this reason that she doesn't think they'll all live together from here on out. She jokes about wanting two kitchens, but it's this sort of design intervention that makes living together possible over the long term.

Unfortunately, many old homes would require such substantial renovations to make them work for multiple generations that many families forgo the investment unless they plan to live together for decades. For example, making a house accessible to elderly grandparents by adding bedrooms to the first floor or making hallways wide enough for a wheelchair can be cost prohibitive.

One designer hoping to change that is Lisa M. Cini, an architect who has lived multigenerationally. Cini lived with her parents, her children, and her grandmother for five years. This experience turned her into an advocate for multigenerational living, after seeing the benefits to her children of having more family around to care for them and seeing how living with her elders made their lives easier. A 2018 study by AARP showed that three out of four adults age fifty or older want to age in place; getting younger generations to move in may be a good way for some seniors to get assisted living without moving.[29]

Cini recently bought a ten-thousand-square-foot house in Columbus, Ohio, that she is turning into a model for multigenerational housing. The home is meant to showcase the latest in technology for seniors, like a kitchen equipped with robots that can prepare food and smart flooring intended to ward off slips and falls. Custom furniture will support seniors who are aging in place.

But for all the work on the house, Cini recognizes that American housing stock isn't as conducive to multigenerational households as what you'd find in other countries. In countries like India and China, many houses are initially built as a single level in concrete. As the children age and need space for their own families, the family builds a second story onto the house. Houses grow vertically and are typically fairly modular, given that they expand as needed to accommodate family members. Additionally, in those countries the culture supports a theory of success that stems from a family's legacy, not the success of individual members. In the United States, "no one has shown the financial value of developing multigenerational housing," Cini says. As a result—and without a kind of asset class for this type of housing—most families will have to undertake their own experiments in multigenerational housing.

While Cini would love to see more newly built multigenerational housing, she recognizes it's an uphill battle. "The sign of success is to leave and never come back. It's not about accumulating family wealth, it's about: How do we get out?"

Cini tells the story of a developer based outside Cincinnati who sought to create a multigenerational housing development. The site was located in the suburbs, where the zoning would have enabled a variety of commercial uses—even a gas station— but to use the site for multigenerational residential was going to require variances. Unfortunately, the community where the site was located was strongly opposed to multigenerational housing, which to the residents had connotations of lower-income and immigrant families. Due to this racist and classist prejudice, community protest against the project ultimately ended up killing it. The developer sold the land. Given the direction of similar parcels, it will most likely become a strip mall.

Until the United States overcomes its fear of diverse communities, it's never going to have the housing options it truly needs.

AARP HAS THE mission of empowering people to choose how they live as they age. Their communications materials typically cover health and financial stability, but recently, livable communities have become a priority. AARP has gotten heavily involved in state housing-policy issues, particularly around accessory dwelling units, which are popular with their members (a 2019 survey conducted by the organization found that seven out of ten adults would like to build an ADU on their property if it could house a loved one).[30] Seeing that it could activate its formidable base around housing, AARP was emboldened to think more broadly about housing solutions that might provide greater affordability and improve livability for seniors.

"The idea is that we just don't have enough options to meet the needs of people, and we need more and better options as we age and shift and change," says Rodney Harrell, vice president of family, home, and community for AARP.

The organization funded and participated in coalitions to support pro-ADU legislation in California, Oregon, and Washington. It was one of the collaborators on a 2017 exhibition at the National Building Museum called *Making Room: Housing for a Changing America*, which looked at co-living, multigenerational housing, and more. In the report that coincided with the exhibition, AARP noted that only about 1 percent of the nation's housing in 2017 was equipped to meet the needs of seniors.[31]

"We're having people who aren't having their needs met, or who are compromising to fit their lives within their homes, instead of having homes that fit their needs," Harrell says. The problem isn't just the lack of housing tailored to multigenerational families, but the lack of options overall.

"I trace it back to how we developed as a country, especially after World War II," Harrell says. "The suburban development, lots of single-family homes, became the norm and so in a lot of places we don't have the duplexes and triplexes and other forms of housing that were made for multiple families, and multiple types of households that include multigenerational families."

How should cities and states solve that problem? AARP's answer is an overall prescription for more housing choices. While aging successfully has long been synonymous with independence, AARP is among the organizations pushing to rethink this as interdependence, which is critical to the success of multigenerational housing. As Mike Healy's story illustrates, old housing types that are already zoned for two- or three-family homes are great multigenerational housing options. To that end, AARP is backing "missing middle" housing initiatives around the country, which promote the importance of housing types between standalone single-family homes and dense apartment buildings.

But for AARP, the solutions can't just be about improving the single-family home for generations of a family with different needs. Rather, the organization is more focused on cutting-edge solutions. It has commissioned a report about countries around the world, like Singapore and Germany, that not only have high levels of multigenerational housing but actually incentivize it. The hope is that AARP can learn from some of those ideas and help them get traction here in the United States.

To give one example, AARP is funding the University of Southern Indiana to study six-hundred-square-foot modular houses from Japan called Minka homes to understand the potential of senior-friendly ADUs. If affordable, easy to build, and focused on senior needs, these homes could potentially enable more multigenerational households with backyard cottages. The not-yet-trend already has a cute name: PIMBYs, a play on the common terms NIMBY and YIMBY. PIMBYs are "parents in my backyard."

COMPARED TO A trend like co-living, multigenerational housing, intergenerational living, and grandfamilies are just not sexy. They touch on issues of human vulnerability and the need for caregiving—subjects that many prefer to push aside. Indeed, for the past half century, families have increasingly pushed their young and their old out of sight, paying someone else to take care of them. Whether in swanky fifty-five-plus residencies or in nursing homes, the elderly have been segregated into their own communities, and American work schedules have made day care for children ever more essential. There are great benefits to outsourcing this work, and for those without strong family units eldercare and childcare are essential services. But both have wildly increased in cost in the past decade. Multigenerational housing could be at least part of the solution for some families.

Here's the rub: Embracing multigenerational housing requires more than changing the housing type or zoning. It means changing how we engage with our families and with aging. Are we ready to do that? I am reminded of something that Jane Marie O'Connor said in our conversation: "We don't stay the same age; we are all marching forward. God willing, we're marching forward." Aging is tough. Family members can be hard to deal with. But as Mike Healy's story illustrates, there's an upside to acknowledging mortality that, far from depressing or disrupting families, can actually bolster them. We need institutions from all sectors to better accommodate caregiving and recognize the huge role that housing choices—and options—play in that.

CHAPTER SEVEN

HOUSING THAT HEALS

THE KENSINGTON NEIGHBORHOOD OF Philadelphia has the ignominious reputation of being the epicenter of the city's opioid crisis. Once a hub of manufacturing with working-class residents, today Kensington struggles with a 60 percent poverty rate and high rates of violence, unemployment, and drug use. Many entities—from local government to community-development organizations, public schools to universities—are fighting alongside residents for a better future. One such organization is Shift Capital, a social-impact-driven real estate development company that has made a name for itself by renovating more than 260,000 square feet in a former textile complex to serve as studio space for artists and entrepreneurs. As part of its investment in the neighborhood, Shift also owns about one hundred homes across Kensington.

Despite all of Kensington's drawbacks, the area stands to become gentrified in the next decade. It's just blocks from Fishtown and Port Richmond, areas that have seen scores of new developments. Shift is hoping to steer Kensington to a future as a mixed-income neighborhood with less intergenerational poverty, using real estate as a lever to restore safety and vitality, and as a hedge against displacement. For Shift's vision to succeed, maintaining a good relationship with tenants, and understanding their needs, is going to be critical.

Shift's cofounder, Brian Murray, describes himself as "a community-development person at heart," which he says comes with "a mindset of how real estate touches people's lives." Most renters think of their landlord as a distant or abstract entity; Murray sees the landlord-tenant relationship as something far-reaching. "I've always viewed the property management world as an untapped delivery system," he says. Developers selling new housing aren't incentivized to provide healthier homes unless it's part of the market demand. But for landlords, the relationship with residents continues after the lease is signed. Landlords also have the opportunity to deliver services to their tenants beyond typical appliance repairs or utilities. Shift already serves as a conduit for education, alerting tenants to job fairs and other opportunities, and provides some basic safety tools, like security cameras. But Murray wanted to do more.

In 2019, Murray was approached by entrepreneur Matt Hoffman, who had recently launched a social impact fund called HousingTech Ventures. Hoffman proposed a program called HEALTH+, which would give tenants in Shift Capital's one hundred properties access to telemedicine and low-cost prescriptions. Telemedicine offers a convenient health-care option for people seeking to avoid the hassles of booking appointments in advance or even the time spent in a waiting room. And in the age of the COVID-19 pandemic, telemedicine has become a critical way for people to get medical care without risking infection in a hospital or doctor's office. At $10 per month, the service costs about as much as two adults taking a bus to the doctor's office and back. But the real advantage is that telemedicine can be far more convenient and quicker for patients than a visit to an urgent care clinic.

Shift's renters are entirely low-income. A good chunk are single mothers with children, getting by month to month. For many, a trip to the doctor means missing work, which may mean missing out on pay or even facing penalties for calling in sick. Many more may never take themselves or their sick children to the doctor simply because there's no time for it in their schedule. Imagining the time and money that tenants could potentially save by enrolling in the program, Murray felt it was a no-brainer to offer it.

Murray is motivated by the notion that this is a meaningful amenity to his renters and something that will keep his tenants loyal. But there may also be a business case for keeping his renters healthy. For many people, just one sickness can become a slew of cascading consequences. Being sick can lead to missed work, which leads to missed rent, which leads to eviction, which leads to any number of bad outcomes. If Murray's renters stay healthy, employed, and in their homes, he may be less likely to have to deal with turnover, which affects his bottom line.

Murray admits it's a pretty weak business case, at least until there are data to prove that the telemedicine service has a measurable impact on tenant stability (something he plans to study over the next few years). Murray isn't sure how many people will sign up, what the usage will be like, or if his hunch that this program can help people withstand other difficulties in life will pan out. But he does know that in a neighborhood like Kensington, it is a small step toward keeping people healthy. He hopes other landlords will consider how they can affect their tenants' lives for the better. "My dream is that this inspires others to do it," Murray says.

Landlords and developers are now beginning to think about providing health care as an amenity in the same way they once thought about providing cable or a cleaning service. While a simple telemedicine program like HEALTH+ is the most basic way to integrate health into housing, other developers are going much deeper. Some developers come from a unique vantage point: they're health insurance companies or health-care institutions like hospitals. They have a window into health needs and solutions that the typical residential developer lacks, and are using that insight to tackle the hard problems of homelessness and other acute health conditions. Others are coming to wellness by sourcing the needs and wants of their clientele and looking at how to provide a housing experience that supports healthy living.

Like co-living and multigenerational residences, health-driven housing is not an entirely new trend. After all, single-family homes were originally touted as an escape from the crowded, unsanitary tenements, and as a way to ensure children access to nature, play space, and a private family life (all of which were seen as critical to physical and mental health). But while this style of housing may have had benefits over shared living in the late nineteenth and early twentieth centuries, today those who live in single-family homes in the suburbs are no better off than their peers in cities.

The characteristics of healthy communities have dramatically changed in recent decades. Instead of the suburb that prioritizes separate houses in purely residential areas, healthy communities today are those that give people the ability to walk to daily amenities, neighborhood commerce, local food sources, community recreation facilities, and shared green spaces. Places that have all these attributes plus affordability are frustratingly rare, but as the trend of building intentionally healthy communities takes hold, and as governments prioritize health in their investments, these attributes are bound to spread to more housing and neighborhoods.

We're already starting to see new developments around the country putting a health-promoting lifestyle front and center, listing it as the top priority for their residents. Some of these communities are more spa than city, and access to them is limited to the wealthy few. Others, developed by health-focused nonprofits like hospitals and health insurers, are genuinely aimed at homeless and low-income tenants.

These trends pose a set of tantalizing questions: What if the best way to address today's common health concerns wasn't with new medicines but with new approaches to housing? What if health and wellness drove value in the housing industry rather than prestige and privacy? What if the American Dream for housing wasn't just a yearning for the financial boon that homeownership provides, but also for a home that was a source of mental and physical health? A new set of housing developers are answering these questions and reckoning with the ways that single-family housing has caused the health crises of today.

IN 2016, A startling thing happened: average life expectancy in the United States declined. It continued to go down for the next three years, the longest such decline since 1918, when World War I and the Spanish flu caused young deaths that dramatically drove down the statistical average.

For most of American history, each generation presumed it would have a better economic and health outlook than the one that came before. Now here was evidence that life was actually getting worse for contemporary Americans.

What exactly was driving the decrease in average life expectancy? Many of the traditional major causes of death, like heart disease, were still declining. The shortened average life span was attributed to something broadly called "deaths of despair." Predominantly affecting middle-aged white people who had suffered economic hardships, these deaths were driven by drug and alcohol addiction and included overdoses and liver disease. Death by suicide was also on the rise. While the trend began in 1998, it accelerated more recently as opioid prescriptions and overdoses dramatically increased and worsened life outcomes.[1]

The findings prompted a widespread debate about quality of life for Americans. There was not only the obvious crisis of the opioid epidemic, but there were also studies showing that, even among the general population, the percentage of Americans self-reporting unhappiness had gone up since the 1990s.[2] Young adults had rising levels of anxiety and increased rates of antidepressant prescriptions. As more people found themselves in front of their screens at home and less frequently interacting in real life, social isolation and loneliness had become more prevalent. One study showed that loneliness was as bad for you as smoking cigarettes because of the way it correlated negatively with a host of mortality factors.[3] Additionally, rates of obesity and diabetes had plateaued in 2005–2006, but by 2016 were on the rise again.[4]

No matter how you looked at it, Americans were struggling. Politicians, health-care professionals, and the general public all debated what was making us less happy and healthy. Food choices, prescriptions, and culture all played a role. But a body of research pointed to the ways that unaffordable, isolating, dilapidated, and unsafe housing could have a deleterious effect on people's health too.

Health policy and housing policy are being linked today in a way they haven't been before, and it has major consequences for how an array of nonprofits, governments, and philanthropies do business. In recent years, health-policy advocates have focused on the social determinants of health: the ways that housing, education, employment, and access to amenities play a role in health outcomes. At the same time, housing advocates have been exploring the four main pathways through which housing can affect health: stability, safety, affordability, and neighborhood.

There is a strong correlation between stable housing and health. As one would expect, chronic homelessness leads to a series of health disadvantages, but even frequent moves, couch surfing, and falling behind on rent have been shown to correlate with poor health outcomes among youth, such as depression, drug use, and higher rates of teen pregnancy.[5] A study by the Providence Center for Outcomes Research and Education, based in Portland, Oregon, found that moving housing-unstable people into stable, affordable housing reduced their Medicaid expenditures by 12 percent.[6]

Home safety is something that many people in middle- or upper-income neighborhoods take for granted, but in low-income neighborhoods there are often many risks in the home. Lead, in the form of lead paint or in old pipes that leach into water systems, can cause irreversible damage to young children's developing brains. Buildings with deferred maintenance, where ventilation systems are not properly functioning and mold may have grown, can trigger asthma. Locations with poor air quality—near refineries or other industrial operations, for example—lead to higher asthma and cancer rates. Likewise, living in a neighborhood with unkempt vacant lots, high crime rates, high-volume roads, and no safe places to exercise has been shown to trigger stress and lead to a less healthy life.

Finally, numerous studies have shown that affordability is literally a lifesaver. People who spend less on housing costs have more money to spend on food and medical care. The landmark government study on the effects of living in a high-poverty neighborhood, "Moving to Opportunity," showed that mental-health gains, rather than economic gains, were among the most important advantages of moving to a less-poor neighborhood.[7]

That quality housing is the foundation for health has been a popular notion for decades among homelessness advocates who promote a "housing first" philosophy. Housing first is the idea that until homeless people are properly housed, they cannot address their mental and physical needs or take on educational or employment opportunities. That vision has lately been adopted beyond homelessness and is informing how health-care providers, governments, philanthropies, and nonprofits address human health in a holistic way.

To give one example, California governor Gavin Newsom dedicated the entirety of his 2020 State of the State address to housing and homelessness. In the speech, he aptly noted, "Health care and housing can no longer be divorced. After all, what's more fundamental to a person's well-being than a roof over their head? Doctors should be able to write prescriptions for housing the same way they do for insulin or antibiotics."[8] The way that health-care providers are jumping into developing housing, this hope may become a reality in the coming decades.

Newsom need look no further than his home state, where Kaiser Permanente is showing just how involved a health-care institution can get with housing. The managed-care provider—with $80 billion in annual revenue, more than two hundred thousand employees, and over twelve million members—has long supported nonprofit organizations that provide the vulnerable with housing. Now it's taking its influence and money in a new direction through a partnership with Enterprise Community Partners.

Enterprise is an East Coast–based community-development organization that, over the course of nearly four decades, has built hundreds of thousands of units of affordable housing. With Kaiser Permanente's funding, they have established two new entities to create health-driven housing: a Housing for Health Fund, which will provide up to $85 million in equity (aka cash) toward building new housing in Northern California, and the RxHome Fund, a $100 million revolving loan fund to enable housing developments across Kaiser Permanente's footprint (a range of states from Hawaii to Colorado to Maryland), targeting low-income or special-needs individuals and families.

What's most distinct about the work Kaiser Permanente and Enterprise are doing is the Health Action Plan that is part of each project. Enterprise, along with the US Green Building Council and the Health Impact Project, created the Health Action Plan process as a road map to guide developers and their constituents in understanding the health implications of housing choices. A typical housing development process involves architects and engineers, but otherwise has no engagement with professionals who take human health into account. However, the Health Action Plan ensures each development goes through a process of assessments from public-health professionals, discussions at public meetings, and feedback from the intended resident population. As a result, the developers are able to produce interventions that attempt to address residents' health needs.[9]

While the Kaiser Permanente and Enterprise partnership could ostensibly support many types of housing, their focus has been on creating housing for homeless people. According to Brian Rahmer, vice president of health and housing at Enterprise, Kaiser Permanente is far from the only health-care institution developing housing for this population. Following the passage of the Affordable Care Act, health-care providers are now required to screen patients for social needs beyond the hospital's walls. "How do we make sure that our patients, if we identify them as homeless, have the connections to resources for shelters or supportive housing?" Rahmer asks. "That has been where a lot of effort from the health-care sector has been focused, particularly around forming partnerships in that space."

Rahmer gives the example of the partnership between Denver Health and the Denver Housing Authority. Homeless people are often the most frequent users of a hospital's emergency room; hospitals in turn can be required to host them until they can be safely discharged to a shelter. Denver Health was no exception, with numerous homeless patients stuck in limbo in the hospital—including one who had been there for more than 1,500 days. In situations like this, many hospitals are finding it's cheaper to build housing for homeless patients than to keep them in hospital beds.

Denver Health identified an old, unused office building on its campus and sought to turn it into a combination of affordable

senior housing and apartments for homeless people transition-
ing out of the hospital. Denver Health then sold the building and leased the land to the local housing authority, which
put together sources of funding to renovate and repurpose the
building. A bed at the Denver Health hospital is $2,700 per
night; housing a homeless person could cost just $10,000 per
year in one of these new units.

This idea of hospitals helping to solve the homelessness
crisis is catching on, big time. The New Jersey Housing and
Mortgage Finance Agency (NJHMFA) is another entity that
has seen the benefits of turning hospitals into developers. Prior
to joining NJHMFA, the agency's director, Charles Richman,
ran the New Jersey Department of Community Affairs (DCA),
where he led a pilot program in Camden County that helped
house the area's most frequent users of hospital emergency
rooms. The program was a true win-win: it added housing supply to the area, helped people who are frequently hospitalized
and housing unstable manage their conditions, and helped
reduce costs for local hospitals.

At the same time, DCA initiated a program to support hospitals in developing "anchor institution" strategies. Anchor institutions are entities like hospitals, universities, or large museums
that are unlikely to move (thus, anchored in the city) and have
opportunities to benefit their neighborhoods through employment, procurement, real estate development, and other activities.
Anchor institution theory has caught on among this group, and
many hospitals intentionally coordinate their investment priorities, procurement practices, and community benefits. Housing
the homeless fits within that strategy, as it aligns the hospital's
contribution to the community with controlling costs.

At NJHMFA, Richman was able to combine these two ideas into a subsidy program that would incentivize hospitals to build a small number of affordable housing units for frequent hospital users. The program is supported by a subsidy of up to $4 million, a mortgage directly linked to the program, and a match from the hospital in land or other resources. It is, therefore, able to generate not only housing but a suite of other supportive services for residents.

New Jersey has six hospitals with projects in the pipeline. St. Joseph's Hospital in Paterson, New Jersey, has already broken ground on a $20 million project that is expected to generate seventy-one units of housing for no- to low-income residents.

It makes sense that, as developed countries grapple with an epidemic of unhealthy residents, hospitals would seek to play a role in solving the problem. Recognizing that housing is critical to health, they have extended their mission to keep people healthy into the home. And they've found a way to develop housing while improving their bottom line. But what took hospitals so long to see their potential as developers?

Charles Richman says that hospital executives aren't accustomed to thinking of their institutions this way. While practitioners see an obvious connection between health and housing, the balance sheet of hospitals wouldn't clearly suggest it. Additionally, developing housing and understanding how to match units to patients requires a different skill set—even different employees—than the conventional work of treating people with illnesses.

Hospitals that see themselves as the new housing developers have the potential to benefit many different kinds of people. Foremost, the residents of the units benefit—the homeless and housing-insecure people who finally have a stable place to call home. But there are myriad benefits for hospitals too. First, they're able to fulfill their mission and treat patients with the "prescription" of housing in a way that medicine and other interventions cannot. Second, they can free up their emergency-room beds for other patients, which not only reduces wait times and improves the experience for occasional ER users but also provides hospitals with more opportunities to get paid for those visits. Third, cities get the benefits of having fewer homeless people in their shelters, gaining more development (which generates construction jobs), and responsibly getting homeless people off the streets.

There's also another big connection between hospitals and homelessness: many people lose their jobs when fighting a serious illness, such as cancer, and as a result can become homeless. Once a breadwinner loses his or her job, it often takes months to get a disability. In the meantime, the family may be evicted or lose their house to foreclosure. The nexus of homelessness and illness applies to a far larger group than one might imagine, and hospitals are uniquely positioned to know who among their patients are at risk of homelessness and to intervene. Indeed, one could imagine that hospitals, insurers, and other health-care institutions will eventually expand beyond serving the homeless and focus on the elderly or other groups of people whose health is particularly dependent on housing.

For too long, the hospital-to-shelter cycle simply perpetuated and prolonged the hospital's involvement in treating homeless people. As these projects prove, housing them can (surprise!) help these people heal in ways that temporary, unstable housing cannot.

But we've yet to see hospitals invest in the kinds of comprehensive services that homeless people truly need. For some, a suite of mental and physical health care is paramount, but for others, education, job opportunities, and soft-skills training may be most useful. It remains to be seen if the hospitals getting into housing will see their work ending with a key to an apartment, or if they will take on these other services that many nonprofits focused on sheltering the homeless provide.

Ultimately, hospitals and health-care institutions are shifting from a more reactive approach to a more preventative one. The Children's Hospital of Philadelphia (CHOP), for example, launched a pilot project in 2018 to better understand the relationship between housing and childhood asthma. The Community Asthma Prevention Program Plus addresses CHOP's neighboring area of West Philadelphia, where one in four children has the condition.

Since 1997, CHOP has had a program that provides home visits to patients with chronic asthma in order to assess any environmental causes. That program alone has resulted in a 50 percent drop in hospitalizations for participants.[10] Now, in a partnership with the Philadelphia Housing Development Corporation, CHOP is remediating one hundred homes to address mold, pest infestations, carpet, or other environmental factors deemed to be a cause of asthma. As part of the program, an air monitor, and a dehumidifier if necessary, will be installed in each home. The goal is to reduce a number of key indicators: emergency-room visits, hospital stays, missed days of school and work, and health-care costs.

How might this line of work expand to other conditions? One could imagine hospitals and health-care providers developing in-home programs intended to prevent or help manage a range of diseases, from diabetes to cancer to depression. But what if we changed our communities to make them healthier from the start?

NAME A MAJOR city, and you will find there is a neighborhood dominated by a big health institution. These hospitals often spawn transportation infrastructure like shuttles and lure people to live nearby, but rarely is there a wellness focus in the community. That is changing, as dozens of medical institutions recognize an opportunity to extend their mission into their communities, and especially into homes.

Rochester is Minnesota's third-largest city, with just more than one hundred thousand residents. But it draws three million visitors a year—far more than the average city of that size does—because it is home to the renowned Mayo Clinic. People from around the world come to Rochester to partake in the Mayo Clinic's cutting-edge services. Increasingly, its model for outpatient care involves not just follow-up visits but a transformation of a patient's lifestyle. What if, instead of sending a patient home as quickly as possible, the next step to recovery involved living in Rochester and adapting to a wellness-oriented lifestyle?

The city is now participating in a public-private partnership to invest more than $5 billion over twenty years to center the city around goals of "hope, health, and hospitality." Another H: housing. Called the Destination Medical Center (DMC), the massive complex calls for somewhere between 2,200 and 3,100 new housing units—mostly multifamily, in line with nearby Minneapolis's progressive stance against exclusionary zoning for single-family housing. For the Mayo Clinic's part, it wants healthy housing to attract and retain the best possible talent at its own facilities.[11]

The DMC takes the approach that housing is just one part of creating a healthy community. A neighborhood can have a variety of physical and mental impacts. To that end, the DMC will feature a bike loop that goes through the city and transportation that offers people with disabilities greater access. The DMC will also prioritize cultural offerings, like community gatherings downtown and a renovated theater. A linear park called Discovery Walk that connects downtown to a life-sciences campus to a city park will encourage walking through DMC neighborhoods.

That said, this hoped-for vision has already met some tough realities about the downsides of new development. The DMC is hoping to lure not just patients and medical practitioners but also medical entrepreneurs and biotech companies. The DMC's website and promotional materials heavily focus on how it will be a hub of medical innovation, a kind of Silicon Valley in the Midwest. Already, the DMC has a population and investment growth rate that far exceeds the rest of the region in Minnesota. Many employees of the DMC live not downtown but in nearby suburbs, and as a result housing prices in the neighboring counties have increased. While the city is focused on building a community, its housing may look more like the hospitality industry. The amenities conjure an image of vacation or rehab more than enhanced daily life. There's little mention of public schools or corner stores in this vision. That said, you could imagine how other hospitals around the country could build upon this model of taking a medical institution out of its four walls and into neighborhoods.

While the DMC hints at one way for communities around the country to put health at the center of their planning, wellness communities aimed at people searching for a healthier lifestyle are another.

It is not a stretch to say that much of modern American life is unhealthy. Whether in a city or in the suburbs, most adults spend their days in desk jobs that require them to sit for eight hours a day, staring at a screen, often in office buildings with inoperable windows and stark overhead lighting. Commuting is a traffic- and rage-filled drive, a noisy subway commute, or a potentially life-threatening bike ride (just 2.7 percent of Americans walk to work). People spend more than three hours a day on their cell phones, an experience that raises cortisol in many. Blue light from our myriad screens has been shown to damage the mitochondria in our DNA. Many of us eat processed or factory-farmed foods, both of which correlate with illnesses like diabetes and heart disease. And some 40 percent of Americans don't get the recommended minimum of seven hours of sleep per night.

At the same time, the very basics of quality air and water have been threatened in a number of communities across the country. A 2019 study showed that American cities are now experiencing worse air quality, after many years of improvements. Higher numbers of wildfires, lowered environmental regulations, and economic changes account for much of the uptick. Increased pollution has been known to contribute to cognitive declines, and in cases of severe air pollution it has been shown to decrease life expectancy. Many older industrial cities—from Flint to Newark to Baltimore—have been grappling with lead in their water, a crisis that threatens the health of their youngest generations. Our communities are struggling with pollution in ways thought to have been solved decades ago.

Most city governments are cognizant of the role they play in their residents' health. In addition to the public-health programs that ensure basic health and safety for the entire range of citizens, quality-of-life improvements have increasingly come to the fore. Cities are going beyond parks and recreation centers, working hard to expand access to waterfronts and programmed public spaces, or creating taxes on sweetened beverages and seeking to protect waterways through plastic-bag bans. But these are measures that merely work at the edges of unhealthy contemporary lifestyles.

So it's no wonder that many people are seeking an overhaul— or a rejection—of the contemporary American lifestyle. While some are flocking to tiny homes or co-living, others are looking to places focused on health and wellness, without many of the distractions and downsides of modern-day life.

Harvest by Hillwood is a so-called agri-hood, "with a rustic affection for the simple life, where farm-to-table gardening inspires neighbors to Grow Together and live a bountiful life," according to their website.[12] Residents of the community get to grow their own produce, garden with the community, take on-site agriculture classes, and share their surplus food with the North Texas Food Bank.

The website for EcoVillage in Ithaca, New York, tells visitors searching for an intentional community to look no further. Composed of three cohousing villages, EcoVillage has more than two hundred residents, approximately one-fifth of whom are retirees. Here, residents typically volunteer two to three hours per week toward the community's upkeep, cars are parked

essentially marrying the best of the suburbs with the best of village life.

Here, all the homes are sited close to the street, and most of them have front porches to encourage interaction with passersby. Residential and retail are connected, with apartments located above and adjacent to stores. All of the retail embodies Serenbe's ethos of being active (a bike store, a yoga studio) and living conscientiously (a Montessori preschool, a bookstore). All the small neighborhoods within the development are in walking distance of one another, sometimes along nature trails. Serenbe Farms, a gorgeous organic farm run by a sole farmer named Ian, features rows of lettuce, beets, and peppers and a shitake-mushroom grove growing on dead wood in the shade. Ian talks about how the farm produce is "my contribution to health care" for Serenbe residents. Having tasted some of the fresh produce in my salad at a local restaurant just moments before, I could see how this resource would truly nourish residents.

Serenbe's approach to community planning is highly intentional and purposefully communal: no house has a large backyard, so families are encouraged to use shared public spaces like the town green, swimming pool, and public gazebos. In one of the neighborhoods, there's a footpath behind a row of houses where you can imagine impromptu chatting between neighbors. The town is set up to encourage this kind of random interaction, stimulating the kind of see-and-be-seen nature of city life that the suburbs—with their drive-in garages—were built against.

More than anything else, Serenbe lives up to its name: the place is quiet and serene. Cars are so infrequent that you can walk in the streets. As I meandered around town, a thirtysomething father with his son sitting on his shoulders led a tour for prospective residents entirely through traffic lanes. There are occasional buzz saws of construction under way, but the place is largely devoid of the deafening volumes you experience even in more mature suburbs.

As I walked or drove through the neighborhoods, I felt a sense of boredom creeping over me. Who could live somewhere with just three restaurants and three clothing stores? Then I realized: That's kind of the point. Serenbe is a rejection of the overstimulating life we've made for ourselves in almost every context.

On my night in Serenbe, I hoped to attend a concert by an avant-garde bluegrass-meets-classical duo named Violet Bell. It was a public concert held in a private home, open to anyone who happened to read about the event. A crowd of thirty people edged into one of the town's cottages. As a line formed, I lost my interest in going inside—opting instead for a walk in the crisp night air and the chance to see stars.

I was staying in a small carriage-house ADU listed on Airbnb. (One admirable aspect of Serenbe's new construction is how many of the houses are built with ADUs attached.) Lauren and Josh, a thirtysomething couple from Toms River, New Jersey, had just moved into the main house next door four months earlier. As Lauren explained, her decision to move to Serenbe was brought on by boring, isolating winters with her children. Every winter, Lauren would feel the same sense of depression, so she began taking road trips south with her family. They drove around North Carolina—Raleigh-Durham, Asheville, Greenville—looking for the right place to move. But none of these cities were the right fit—and actually some of them had cold winters too. The last stop was a night at the Inn at Serenbe—the kind of picturesque rural inn that serves as the perfect backdrop for a country wedding. Immediately, she called the family's search off. She had found her new community.

If the winters prompted her to leave New Jersey, the idea of finding a community is what brought her to Serenbe. During her first summer in Serenbe, she would sit on her rental's porch and neighbors would stroll by and stop to chat. On Halloween, there was a block party that everyone was invited to. Other moms frequently offer to look after kids or do group activities. One night, her husband cut the tip of his finger off. As she stood outside on her phone trying to call an urgent-care clinic, a neighbor who works as a medic came up and asked how he could help. These interactions are nothing extraordinary; rather, they could be defined as "weak ties," the kinds of acquaintance-level relationships that make up the bulk of human interaction. But research has shown that weak ties contribute to a sense of social and emotional well-being, and that they're lacking in many neighborhoods that don't intentionally cultivate a sense of community.[13]

Another plus for Lauren's family is that the outdoor spaces are made for young kids, but no one stays in their own backyard. A patch used as a medicinal herb garden in the summer flows down to a bocce court. Paths weave in and out of backyards, encouraging kids to ramble on their own. On the town green, there's a sunken trampoline where I saw a rotating cast of kids spend hours jumping and playing. The inn has a livestock-feeding area and horses that nuzzle the palms of passersby.

Yes, Serenbe can get a little boring. Lauren and her family go to Atlanta or out of town every week. And, yes, it's lacking a good supermarket and pharmacy, so they stock up on supplies while out of town. But it far outweighs a New Jersey winter. Lauren's parents and brother, who all live in New Jersey, have come to visit and quickly became enamored. Her brother and his wife will be moving into the carriage house in the next month. "The experience speaks for itself," Lauren says.

I can see why. Serenbe is like a life hack: a way to buy into a frankly made-up world of nice places and people that really doesn't extend beyond the community's acreage. It's a fitting demonstration for our times, when the only appropriate response to so many communities struggling with a host of social and environmental challenges might be to reject and ignore them. But although living in a curated community may have its appeal, it's hard to imagine how Serenbe's model could transcend its exclusive nature and become a phenomenon that works for people of all budgets.

That said, there are ways to take elements of Serenbe's success and implement them elsewhere to still reap the health benefits. For one thing, Serenbe shows just how much aesthetics—not typically a concern in public housing or even in many commercial ventures these days—matter. How much do loud noise, whizzing cars, and the twenty-four-seven nature of our communities take a toll on people's health? Serenbe shows that communities can more seriously address the ways that contemporary life drains our mental and physical wellness. Cities should take heed; there are ways to limit the bombarding nature of screens advertising at every subway stop or in the backseat of every taxi. They can do more to regulate noise and air pollution. They can take seriously the move to pedestrianize more streets and encourage more walkable neighborhoods. Much as women began noting the undervalued emotional labor they often do in relationships and in family care, perhaps we should begin noting the undercurrent of unhealthy triggers in many of our communities. If we do, we might consider what other efforts would limit sensory overload and restore opportunities for serenity in our own communities.

It's clear that health care is no longer limited to what happens in the doctor's office. With housing as the platform and vehicle for service delivery, we could shift our policies away from pure social or economic benefit to ensure Americans' health. You can get a tax deduction for making your house more energy efficient. Why not have a similar deduction for making your house healthier? Removing asthma triggers, lead paint and pipes, and pests could all become tax-deductible expenses. Likewise, insurance policies often reimburse customers for going to the gym. What if insurers reimbursed you for your civic-association membership or other efforts that build social capital? Finally, are there ways to incentivize people to live in walkable neighborhoods or near public transit, given the health benefits of those neighborhoods?

Brian Rahmer of Enterprise Community Partners notes that we are increasingly seeing how individual health is tied to that of our neighborhoods, which is tied to the health of the planet. "Housing historically has been a place where wealth was generated, a more transactional element of our lives, as opposed to a foundational aspect of what makes us [human] and allows us to bond as human beings and as part of a community," he explains. The idea that housing makes us who we are has always been part of the American Dream. But as we've focused on the financial upside of housing—that idea of "making it"—we've lost sight of how housing informs our health as well.

PART THREE

HOW TO GET THE HOUSING WE WANT

CHAPTER EIGHT

DISRUPTING HOUSING POLICY, INDUSTRY, AND ADVOCACY

I N 2020, AS THE world battles COVID-19, many people are talking about the last comparable global pandemic, the 1918 flu. Approximately one-third of the world's population became infected with the virus, and some 675,000 Americans died as a result. Nineteen-eighteen was also notable as the year that the "Own Your Own Home" campaign launched, encouraging Americans to invest in single-family homeownership and disperse from the city. As already discussed in Chapter Two, there were many financial and social reasons why people moved to the suburbs. But one other reason the suburbs became so popular in the wake of 1918 was that standalone, single-family homes inherently encouraged social distancing that could help people avoid diseases like that vicious flu.

COVID-19 has shown a century later how viruses do not discriminate by housing type, and yet the media is once again ready to impugn cities. Even the *New York Times* has fallen prey to disparaging density and linking it to the virus's exponential spread in New York City: "Many New Yorkers live in high-rises. Sidewalks are crowded. Subways can be jammed. The city has 27,000 residents per square mile, far surpassing the second densest city, San Francisco, with 18,000 per mile."[1] But as the Brookings Institution and others have noted, New York and San Francisco's outbreaks had less to do with density than with policy approaches to the pandemic and economic differences. San Francisco's lockdown happened faster, they tested more people more quickly, and their major employers discouraged going into work.[2] San Francisco is also a wealthier city, and as outbreaks in even less-dense cities like New Orleans and Detroit have shown, poverty is essentially an underlying condition, like hypertension and obesity, correlated with death from COVID-19. Much denser cities in Asia—such as Manila, Tokyo, and Taipei—have avoided becoming overwhelmed by the virus because of their intense testing and tracing efforts.

The *Times* has also gone on to publish articles about New Yorkers fleeing for the suburbs. Between March 15 and April 28, 2020, moves from New York to suburbs in the tristate area were all up over the same period a year ago (as much as 74 percent in Connecticut, 48 percent in New Jersey, and 38 percent in Long Island), according to FlatRate Moving.[3]

Despite the bad press, COVID-19's next victim is unlikely to be cities. Rather, an array of housing options that better accommodate economic hardship, multigenerational families, healthier lifestyles, and digital nomadism is more necessary than ever.

Steven Dietz—founder and CEO of United Dwelling, which converts garages into ADUs (see Chapter Five)—said to the real estate website Bisnow at the end of March, "All I can say is, despite a reduction of advertising and outreach, overall, in the last two weeks, we are experiencing an increase in our inbound call volume."[4] While Dietz can't say for certain what accounts for the rise in interest, there are a number of potential reasons why ADUs are appealing during the pandemic. Maybe people need to access a new source of income to weather the economic downturn. Maybe ADUs are the perfect way to quarantine near family. Maybe people fear nursing homes, which have suffered outbreaks, and want to build ADUs to house their aging parents. Maybe many college students will not be returning to school, and ADUs could serve as ideal places for young adults.

At the same time, one of the cofounders of co-living business Starcity, Jon Dishotsky, says he is seeing a spike in student residents. Many college students had to move quickly off campus but don't want to invest in a long apartment lease or furniture before returning to school (hopefully) in the fall. Dishotsky also quotes a Starcity member on Twitter: "It's a lot more fun to be cooped up with your friends than isolated in a lonely apartment. Everyone's trying new hobbies like baking and making music and it's making this disaster that much more tolerable."[5]

Multigenerational households, which might have been thought to be more at risk of spreading COVID-19, seem to have higher rates of infection or death only in overcrowded circumstances.[6] Meanwhile, many families are uniting in these uncertain times. Many young, single adults moved home with parents to avoid the loneliness of living in solitude during quarantine. Even whole young families moved in with the grandparents to handle remote work without day care. In just one example of a positive multigenerational experience, Ruth Kogen Goodwin, writing for *HuffPost*, called sheltering in place with her in-laws "amazing" because of the way the grandparents help with looking after her children. She adds that "things have been going so well, I'm starting to become anxious about the end of our stay."[7] More family members living together means that we must find better ways of housing them, with privacy and health in mind.

Finally, COVID-19 has revealed how the hectic pace of life is diminishing our health. Air pollution in the form of nitrogen dioxide has dropped dramatically as car usage and industrial activity have slumped with stay-at-home orders. One early study of Wuhan, China, where COVID-19 originated, showed that the strict lockdown resulted in so much less air pollution that the net health benefits to the population outweighed the rise in deaths due to COVID-19.[8] It is doubtful that, when the pandemic subsides, people will completely forget the joy of breathing cleaner air and experiencing quieter neighborhoods. Or that they will revert to the old norms of ignoring the health and safety of neighbors. More than ever before, health-driven housing will become an urgent priority.

Even in these difficult times, Americans are finding ways to reject the rigidity of the single-family home. When the pandemic subsides, it's clear the fight for more alternatives to the single-family home will continue.

HOW CAN WE get the housing we want? Let us count the ways. Government, the private sector, the media, and individuals can all be agents of change. We will have to push for new, untried innovations. But we also have successful examples of cities and multi-sector coalitions that have expanded housing choices and that merely need to be replicated.

The City of Minneapolis stands out as a great case study of what local government can do to provide more housing options, and at the same time address social, economic, and environmental concerns. It shows how one pioneering municipality can lead the way for other cities and states eager to upend decades of bad zoning restrictions.

Minneapolis's success story began years ago, when Jacob Frey was campaigning to become mayor of the city in 2017. At the same time, the city was grappling with an affordable housing crisis. The median housing price had increased to over $250,000 while wages stagnated. Frey's campaign themes—which included urban agriculture, the arts, and transportation—might have sounded like your typical progressive, urbanist platform. But Frey's approach to affordable housing was different: He wasn't pushing the standard rhetoric of more taxes to fund new units or new subsidies to boost construction. Instead, his campaign emphasized the importance of multifamily zoning to create affordability.

At that time, some 70 percent of Minneapolis was dedicated to single-family zoning (for comparison, just 15 percent of New York City is).[9] This prevalence of single-family zoning meant that most homes for sale or rent were expensive, as they had large lot sizes and lots of square footage. As a result, these homes were unaffordable for many of the people looking for a place to live in Minneapolis—particularly for people of color.

Not only was single-family zoning thwarting the supply of more housing, and, therefore, increasing costs, it was also keeping Minneapolis racially segregated. In 2016, the University of Minnesota launched its Mapping Prejudice campaign, which exposed the strong legacy of redlining in Minneapolis. As of 2017, Minneapolis and Saint Paul had among the lowest rates of African American homeownership of any American city, at 19.8 and 17 percent, respectively.[10] As a result, the Twin Cities also had one of the greatest wealth gaps between blacks and whites.

City officials knew the city couldn't build its way to affordability and integration unless it dramatically changed its zoning laws. As the mayoral race was under way, Minneapolis was engaged in a comprehensive urban-planning exercise. The Minneapolis 2040 plan worked with people in the city over the course of two years to understand how best to achieve a number of goals, such as eliminating economic disparities and creating a clean environment, living-wage jobs, and affordable housing.

Single-family housing wasn't helping the city meet its environmental aspirations either. Single-family zoning ensured that each household had a parking space, which encouraged car use, and all those detached homes spread across large lots made it hard for the city to achieve the kind of density necessary to run an efficient public-transportation system. By contrast, multifamily zoning could allow new developments specifically along transit routes and help cut back on car-related carbon.

The civic-engagement process led the 2040 committee to a radical idea: that all residential zoning should allow triplexes by right. Most zoning in Minneapolis stated that any variance to single-family housing required special permission; by essentially reversing that rule, developers and households interested in multifamily housing wouldn't need to go through a difficult process of getting a property rezoned. With single-family-only zoning off the table, anyone would be able build or convert a property into a multifamily residence without getting tripped up by red tape. Frey adopted the idea as part of his platform and won the mayoral election, along with a cohort of progressive city councilmembers. In 2018, the city council approved the measure twelve to one.

Minneapolis's move was a watershed moment for the ongoing debate about how to create affordable housing and address racial segregation. Not long after Minneapolis made headlines, other cities and entire states sought to follow. Oregon and Washington have banned single-family-only zoning in most of their cities. States as unexpected as Nebraska are actively considering similar legislation. While many elected officials still argue that banning single-family-only zoning may not be the right way to cultivate development for their cities, it does seem to be only a matter of time until the combined issues of affordability, racial equity, and climate change force this onto the agenda of every major city.

Getting rid of single-family-only zoning is also a deft political maneuver. People like to call it a ban on single-family zoning, but most of the time the proposed changes just add more housing options. You can still build single-family homes, but you can also build more densely. In many cases, developers will choose to build denser housing if they can without community or government interference. By upzoning everything at once, turf wars and special interests become less powerful and less likely to thwart widespread progress. Senior housing, student housing, co-living, ADUs, multifamily, multigenerational homes, and affordable housing are all more easily constructed when they're permitted by right. It is a collective advance toward having options.

Another thing that's great: changing zoning essentially doesn't cost anything. In fact, it could result in increased tax revenue from the additional property taxes and income taxes that denser housing brings to a region.

And less restrictive zoning has the potential for bipartisan support. Those who feel frustrated by ever-expanding government administration, regulation, and red tape see this as a win. So do progressives, who see it as a quick path toward affordability and social justice.

Minneapolis's approach was data driven and multifaceted, presenting housing as a means to improve the city, not just the end goal. Advocates were armed with the financial, social, and environmental arguments against single-family-only zoning. As a result, a larger coalition of advocates—like environmental and racial justice groups—came to support the idea. It's a strategy that other cities and groups can use to support more co-living, ADUs, multigenerational housing, and wellness communities.

This kind of citywide or statewide zoning change is not without potential for controversy. Some people will say that by cutting back on zoning restrictions that require community approval, communities will be left out of the development discussion. That developers, who rarely live in the communities where they build, will have too much control over how a neighborhood is built. And anti-gentrification activists may say there's no guarantee that the housing that gets built will be affordable or accessible to longtime community residents.

Fair enough. But from a historical perspective, today's zoning is far more limited than what existed in many cities for decades, and by unlocking the opportunity to build new housing types for the demographics that exist today, our communities are bound to be better off.

Exclusionary zoning, like the single-family-only zoning that exists in so many neighborhoods in major metropolitan areas, no longer works. We can expect to see more cities favor policies like Minneapolis's, because getting rid of exclusionary zoning has many benefits that a diverse set of stakeholders care about.

We can also expect states to take on a role in regulating zoning. California, Oregon, and Washington have recently shown how changes to statewide housing policy can pave the way for local changes to ADU regulations. Oregon passed a historic bill in July 2019 that enabled housing options as dense as fourplexes on land in cities of more than twenty-five thousand residents that had previously been reserved for single-family housing. In October 2019, California governor Gavin Newsom signed eighteen bills focused on tackling the state's housing crisis through faster production and fewer restrictions on ADUs.

States can also serve as partners for creating new housing types outside of major cities. Politicians are often eager to combat social and health problems but rarely see housing innovation as a tool. As rural areas suffer from higher rates of deaths of despair and grapple with the social isolation of seniors, state governments could be useful in identifying or potentially even assembling property for wellness communities. State-level policy also provides opportunities to think regionally about housing affordability. Suburbs and rural areas that smartly develop along transportation corridors and add density through multifamily buildings are primed to benefit from coming demographic shifts in ways that dated, sprawling suburban areas cannot.

Zoning is not a silver bullet, but it is a necessary starting point for any community trying to tackle the intertwined issues of affordability, equity, segregation, and climate change. On this foundation, we can build many other policies and practices that can improve housing choices for people, if only we can look at housing with fresh eyes.

UNDERLYING THE CALLS to revise single-family-only zoning is a concern that the dominant homeownership paradigm no longer works for the majority of Americans. For the past century, the US government has intertwined its goals of household wealth creation, a strong national economy, family well-being, and public education. For a while, it seemed like this was the perfect match of several objectives. But as housing remained segregated, so did our schools—and with inequality in schools, life outcomes are altered. Today, the neighborhood that children grow up in, down to the zip code, is the biggest predictor of their health and wealth. As housing has become more expensive, homeownership's benefits have accrued to a smaller, older, and whiter set of Americans. Limited housing choices and attempts to maintain property values pit households against one another, making our cities battlegrounds, not welcoming communities.

At the same time, homeownership has dramatically shifted from what it once was—a single household buying a property to live in—to, increasingly, a company acquiring property as an asset for other purposes, such as rental income, flipping, or a stable investment. As a greater portion of housing is owned by LLCs, iBuyers such as Zillow and Opendoor that allow homeowners to essentially sell their homes over the internet, and other institutional investors, there will be less available housing for sale. What essentially amounts to price-fixing will become a greater problem. Major companies like Invitation Homes are buying up thousands of single-family homes and altering the market, and tech companies like Zillow are leveraging their massive amount of data to purchase, renovate, and flip houses.[11] So long as homes are commodities, there will be individuals and families who value their properties for emotional reasons and investors who value them for financial reasons. These differing motives will naturally create conflict, and investors are coming out on top more often than not. As companies reap the majority of the financial gains of single-family zoning, it is odd that the government would continue its subsidization of homeownership.

Additionally, as building housing has become more expensive, and as the standard for housing has gotten bigger and more elaborate, it requires more and more funding to subsidize. Local governments have tried to get creative about housing solutions—for example, inclusionary zoning, as previously discussed, or Seattle's attempted head tax on companies like Amazon and Microsoft. But the reality is that these programs aren't creating nearly enough units, and aren't nearly fast enough.

A housing policy that truly sees the demographic and economic landscape of today would center on three key issues: We have to actively transition our policies away from homeownership and single-family homes. We must investigate how best to subsidize people, rather than their property. And we must better understand how to regulate landlords and buyers who own hundreds of properties or more, while finding ways to leverage their scale for good.

What would a federal housing policy look like that didn't assume single-family homes were financially, socially, or environmentally tenable anymore? What financial tools could support wealth creation outside of the thirty-year mortgage? How could we better use the housing we have now? We need a suite of brave new ideas if we're really going to address our current housing paradigm's problems, not just make slight improvements to the status quo.

At the core of the American government's housing policy is the belief that homeownership builds wealth, improves communities, and supports healthy families. But too often this belief goes untested and unquestioned. We must ask, Is homeownership truly creating wealth, or is it merely that Americans have no other way to access low-interest, patient capital? Is homeownership creating safer, better-maintained communities, or is it that homeowners care for building facades and sidewalks out of a financial incentive and affluent neighborhoods tend to be safer? Does homeownership create healthy families, or do affordability, stability, and certainty about monthly expenses support wellness?

While the notion that homeownership generates wealth is generally taken as a given, how can we know if it really does? The median net worth of Americans was $97,300 in 2016, and nearly double for homeowners, but this statistic may be a case of correlation rather than causation. Merely having the money to make a down payment puts people in a different financial class than those who couldn't imagine such a thing.

If homeownership does in fact build wealth for the 65 percent who are homeowners, renters are being left still further behind. Homeownership is out of reach for all but the wealthiest in our major cities, so its benefits are accruing to only them. Why have a government policy that supports this? Ensuring that an entrenched class of wealthy people is further enriched by housing while the country is in the midst of an affordable housing crisis creates a situation where people lose trust in capitalism writ large. And, frankly, who can blame them, when you look at how unequally the gains have been distributed?

Housing think tanks will regularly note that homeownership is one of the best tools to build wealth in communities of color. But homeownership creates wealth in part by passing assets down from one generation to another, compounding the inequities between racial groups. So it's counterproductive that many philanthropies focused on tackling intergenerational poverty uncritically support homeownership as a strategy to overcome wealth disparities. If the current housing paradigm remains unchanged, they're playing an endless game of catch-up.

Is it really true that real estate is the best investment, particularly if one doesn't live in a hot coastal city? While real estate does create wealth for big investors, for the average homeowner it isn't the economic boon that one might expect. For all its purported financial benefits, homeownership often comes with uncertainty and potential peril. The housing bust of 2008 resulted in the loss of millions of homes and trillions of dollars of real estate investments. A housing bust may not be the biggest threat, however. In an era of climate change, millions of homes face rising seas and wildfires. The COVID-19 pandemic shows just how fragile markets are in a globalized world. Beyond these catastrophic losses, there are smaller unexpected events—a roof leak that leads to a major renovation, a boiler or an HVAC system that suddenly quits—that frustrate the financial stability and upside that are supposed to come with homeownership.

We also assume that homeownership creates stable neighborhoods. But, while homeownership was once seen as a way of supporting neighborhoods, we have created too many financial incentives and now view housing not as a social good but as a commodity. As a result, speculative real estate practices like flipping houses and building luxury apartments have led to destabilizing gentrification and displacement.

Despite these downsides, the federal government subsidizes homeownership to the tune of $134 billion each year through various programs. A little more than half of that—some $71 billion—comes from the mortgage interest deduction, while the rest is composed of capital gains and other real estate tax deductions. Housing scholar Matthew Desmond gave one example of how the mortgage interest deduction is overwhelmingly regressive in an article in the *New York Times*:

> In 2014, 1.5 million households earning between $40,000 and $50,000 a year claimed the MID, receiving an average benefit of $14 a month. That same year, 6.5 million households with earnings above $200,000 claimed the MID and enjoyed an average benefit of $391 a month. What this means in aggregate is that households with at least six-figure incomes receive more than four-fifths of the total value of mortgage interest and property-tax deductions.[12]

Let's be brave and acknowledge that our country's homeownership policies need to be majorly reimagined. The 2017 tax reform package reduced the maximum mortgage interest deduction to $750,000. It's a good start toward lowering the mortgage interest deduction or eliminating it entirely.

If we are going to support homeownership, let's find smarter ways of doing it. Let's reenvision public housing as we once did public land. The Homestead Act of 1862 gave 160 acres of land to anyone willing to work it for five years. What if, instead of renting out public housing or privatizing it, the government turned it into co-ops and enabled people to purchase an ownership share in public housing?

What if a program aimed at ADUs let renters—rather than existing homeowners—pay for the construction of an ADU, and then enabled them to purchase a share of the overall property and reap the benefits of its upside? What if our government-sponsored enterprises (Fannie Mae and Freddie Mac) helped develop mortgage products designed to work for multigenerational households or unmarried co-owners of a property, so that more people could buy properties together?

Answering these questions would help put us on a path toward more equitable housing policy. But we should definitely also consider ways to build wealth outside of housing. Right now, a mortgage is the only way that many families can access patient, low-interest, fixed-rate capital. People can't get that same kind of thirty-year mortgage to invest in stocks, their own businesses, or other asset types because they don't have sufficient collateral. We have been so focused on real estate that we have simply ignored many other ways to build wealth that could be more productive for society. Let's reorient our federal programs that encourage homeownership and instead test out new forms of asset building that are accessible to all people and not dependent on neighborhood, credit score, or existing assets.

If we truly prioritized the well-being of people, we would subsidize residents with cash instead of subsidizing housing. This idea of giving people money rather than housing vouchers has taken hold, not only in theory like presidential candidate Andrew Yang's universal basic income concept, but in reality in places like Stockton, California. Stockton is the first city in the country to pilot a small program of giving 125 residents $500 per month for eighteen months. Prior to the COVID-19 pandemic, other cities like Philadelphia were primed to develop their own similar study. As more initiatives like Stockton's are tested throughout the country, we may get a clearer picture of how to support people; likely we will see that people's housing needs can't be fulfilled in a one-size-fits-all fashion, like that of vouchers and public housing.

Finally, we must acknowledge that the housing landscape of 2020 is different than that of even a decade ago. The consolidation of housing developers and owners poses a tremendous risk in the coming years. We are living in a time of economies of agglomeration, where large businesses are able to exploit their scale in ways that smaller businesses simply cannot. While COVID-19 undoubtedly wrecked the finances of small landlords who lost both rent and renters, companies like Blackstone started up new housing-purchasing programs, this time raising $10 billion to buy up property in Europe. Companies like Zillow or Invitation Homes won't go away anytime soon; rather, their success may invite new competition and other major investors into the business of leveraging a cushioned balance sheet and real estate big data.

We must find a way to appropriately regulate these large real estate ventures and turn the best of them into an opportunity. While publicly traded investment companies may not have any motivation to help address housing crises in the cities where they invest, there are signs that co-living providers and other housing start-ups view their opportunity and responsibility differently. And many of these smaller, socially responsible companies are in charge of thousands of housing units across the country. In New York and Atlanta, local housing authorities are partnering with the co-living provider Common to create affordable units. In the Atlanta example, 15 percent of the project's 345 beds will be capped at rates affordable to people earning 80 percent of area median income.[13] Co-living providers have the infrastructure and, crucially, the wide-ranging skill set to do the difficult work of creating a capital stack, assembling financing for properties, and fulfilling programming and communications. This makes co-living providers potentially ideal partners to work with on affordable housing, as well as on amenities that support health and well-being. Not surprisingly perhaps, Common went on to spawn the company Noah Apartments (the brand is a play on the acronym for "naturally occurring affordable housing") in May 2020. Noah Apartments benefits from its parent company's marketing savvy to rent workforce housing at a discount to community leaders like nurses, firefighters, police officers, and teachers. In its first mid-Atlantic markets, prices came in under $1,100 per month. There is potential to better integrate old programs—like Section 8 vouchers—into new products like co-living or Nesterly or United Dwelling. As more companies get into the game of purchasing portfolios of thousands of properties, government will need to find ways to partner with, regulate, or influence this group for society's benefit.

If we move beyond homeownership and single-family homes, the world of affordable housing truly opens up. We may find that rezoning for greater density will generate more housing and more equitable neighborhoods. If we can refocus major federal programs like the mortgage interest deduction, we might better meet the needs of a country that has a decreasing homeownership rate and an increasing number of iBuyers. Shifting the housing paradigm from one dominant model to a multiplicity of housing options will unleash opportunities for more Americans. After COVID-19 is over, there will be an urge to go back to "normal." We should resist that in housing and forge ahead with new ideas that make sense for this century.

PURSUING NEW APPROACHES to solving the housing crisis will require new narratives. Media coverage of real estate and the housing affordability crisis swings between profiles in luxury and extreme hardship, failing to convey the everyday challenge of tough housing choices faced by the vast majority of Americans.

Think of the coverage of tiny houses. Is the first image that springs to mind a twentysomething teacher who lives in an efficient, manufactured home? Or is it something more like the HGTV version, where the pint-size home has been souped-up to look like a miniature Tudor or something out of the pages of *Dwell*? It's trendy to call tiny houses tiny houses, unless you live in one and don't see it as defined by its size. Though many studio apartments are the same size as a tiny house, we don't call studios "tiny apartments." There are a number of other names we could consider for tiny houses. Rebranding home types has precedent: what we once called "trailer homes" are now known as "manufactured housing." "Accessory dwelling unit" is clearly a good and neutral, if uninspired, option. We could call tiny houses what they once were: bungalows. Undoubtedly, tiny home manufacturers and occupants will find the right nomenclature. Maybe it's just a house.

Likewise, co-living is still often branded as "adult dorms," despite the fact that co-living could be a way for cities to create more affordable housing for people of all ages. The phrase is a demeaning and inaccurate portrayal if you take this lifestyle choice seriously or are outside the apparent target demographic of single millennials. For the single mother raising her kids in a co-living building or the widower who has found it a convenient option—or for those who haven't yet imagined that co-living might meet their needs—"adult dorm" isn't a useful descriptor. The media also tends to tease people seeking community in their housing choices. You can barely read the phrase "intentional community" without hearing the snark. Yet, no one blames senior citizens for wanting to live in a communal setting, as somehow we have grown to accept that older people want a built-in social life. For younger people, choosing housing that has some social aspect is framed as yet another way they have failed to launch. But as more people find themselves strapped for time, newly transplanted to cities where they know few people, and desperate for a sense of offline community, the co-living and wellness communities have arisen as a reasonable solution.

The media and public's unease with new housing types is reminiscent of the discomfort that online dating and shopping once caused. But now—when some 40 percent of heterosexual couples getting married each year met online—most of us couldn't imagine treating online dating as an inferior way of meeting potential mates.[14] I don't suspect the media is being intentionally snarky or hurtful, just lazy. Reporters forget that, by using shorthand or previously accepted tropes, they're adding shame and stigma to choosing a slightly different lifestyle.

Likewise, the affordable housing crisis is frequently covered in ways that reinforce stereotypes. While, yes, many of the victims of the crisis are homeless people and people of color, many other groups have suffered as well. Nearly half of the people living in Section 8 housing are children. Eighty-three percent of households using vouchers are female-headed.[15] While California's housing crisis gets a lot of attention, the top eleven housing authorities by number of Section 8 vouchers and public housing units are east of the Mississippi. Nearly one million seniors get assistance from HUD, a number that is bound to increase. It's important to frame publicly subsidized housing as an issue of income inequality, racism, and mental health, but it's equally important to frame it as a women's issue, a children's issue, a senior issue, and a student issue. Moreover, this broader framing could increase public support for these very necessary programs.

Finally, given that the media has been pushing the narrative of the American Dream and the white picket fence for decades, it can be hard to envision what success looks like outside a paradigm of stability and wealth creation. Unfortunately, the twenty-first century is likely to be more virtual and more mobile, as we are threatened by climate change and more people the world over are forced to flee their homes as refugees. Clinging to the traditional vision of having made it is another version of the nostalgia that fuels the Make America Great Again ethos. We can't go back—nor should we. We must instead find ways to promote stories of resilience, of community wealth and well-being, of enjoying life even if it doesn't meet the standards of some glossy, ideal best life.

The media and advertising industries certainly helped to create and perpetuate the positive association between the single-family home, wholesomeness, and life satisfaction. Now, it's time for the media to help educate people on housing issues and develop new narratives about different options. The goal would not be pro-YIMBY or density propaganda, but rather more neutral reporting on housing alternatives. There are many ways to promote a narrative of community prosperity. For example, the phrase "community land trust" has shown up only once or twice a year for the past handful of years in the *New York Times*, while the *Wall Street Journal*'s weekly real estate section is called Mansion. Dozens of magazines and television shows focused on housing reinforce the ideal of accumulating personal wealth over that of shared prosperity; offering more counterpoints to this vision of success would help seed ideas for what a new American Dream could look like.

We are also at a turning point for the private sector. Developers who recognize new trends in American lifestyles and demographics need to find ways to update their products to meet twenty-first-century aspirations. The sooner they do so, the better—not only for the public, but for their own bottom line. The status quo of zoning is being chipped away, and the market for single-family homes is changing. As the government finds ways to encourage more affordability, developers who can smartly create more density and housing choice will be able to meet the demands of both the government and investors.

Finally, we can't discount the importance of individual choices, whether as home buyers, housing advocates, or voters. Increasingly, YIMBY groups across the country have pressed for zoning reforms and helped developers and governments usher in dense housing. They have gotten results. The Yes in My Backyard (YIMBY) Act had bipartisan sponsors and passed the House of Representatives in March 2020. The act calls for reducing minimum lot sizes, spurring the production of housing near transportation, and allowing for duplexes and manufactured homes in areas previously zoned for single-family homes. The act was officially supported by twenty nonprofit organizations, ranging from YIMBY Action to the American Planning Association to the National Association of Home Builders, showing how a coalition of civic-sector groups can influence policy. That said, the act still has to pass the Senate to be made into law.

Individual actions don't need to roll up into federal laws to make a difference. There are so many other opportunities that offer the chance to change the direction of your community. There are zoning hearings to attend to voice support for alternatives to the single-family home. Social media and traditional media offer other venues to challenge the status quo. Finally, there are many local organizations that gather advocates for better housing, and you can join them in their efforts.

THE UNITED STATES in 2020 is in crisis. Thrown completely off course by the COVID-19 pandemic, we are still politically and economically divided. We're in despair over how climate change will affect our future. Concerned about technological advances, like personal data and surveillance, we are also distracted and consumed by our screens. Lonely, unhealthy, stressed, and indebted. It's a bleak picture.

In this election year, we're hearing constant debates over the cost of health insurance and tax loopholes that benefit the wealthy, over the problems of student debt and opioid addiction. These issues are crucially important—full stop. But so is housing. Discussion of this issue has been scant, even though it represents the biggest monthly expense for most people; even though the mortgage interest deduction is one of the country's largest regressive tax loopholes; even though student debt has changed the landscape of housing choices for young people; and even though opioid addiction is a leading cause of homelessness.

It is past time to elevate housing to the position in the national dialogue that it deserves. It is not distinct from the conversations about the economy, about health, about technology, about the environment—it is integral to each of them. The social, mental, and physical well-being of our people, and perhaps our democracy, depends on new solutions to our housing crises.

Moreover, while Democrats and Republicans may not agree on what solutions will improve affordability and quality, housing is an issue that lends itself to bipartisan compromise and action. Deregulating housing restrictions gets Republicans excited, while measures to ensure greater housing affordability make Democrats cheer. Initiatives that achieve both could win over a plurality of politicians.

Of course, our housing problems also cannot be solved by the public sector alone. Go to any planning hearing about a new development, and you will witness how government, developers, YIMBYs, NIMBYs, and nonprofit housing advocates all jostle to influence the direction of cities. Unlike many of the top political issues that require acts of Congress to solve, all residents can play a role in creating better housing options now, rather than years in the future.

This book illustrates the paradigm shift under way, changing characteristics of households and their preferred living situations. In this brave new world, we'll need to reexamine and be prepared for a genuine change in our long-held assumptions about how to solve the housing crisis. We must rethink homeownership as the primary source of wealth creation for Americans, rethink zoning that privileges single-family homes, and rethink the variety of ways the federal government incentivizes and rewards single-family housing. The way we got to unaffordable, unhealthy, and uninspired housing was long and complicated. How we will get out of this mess is unlikely to be quick or easy either.

This is an exciting moment to contemplate the future of housing. Despite decades of inertia, the housing industry, the government, and the public have started to change the kind of housing they build, permit, and live in, because they are beginning to realize that the American Dream of the 1950s does not align with today's world. Housing policies and developments are capable of transforming cities within just a few years. Challenges to single-family zoning are common just a few years after Minneapolis changed its rules. Co-living has spread quickly too. Common, WeLive, and Ollie first established their co-living businesses a handful of years ago. Today, they have collectively raised hundreds of millions of dollars in investment and gone from a fringe phenomenon to a profitable asset class in record time. How much longer until we bridge the gap between co-living for millennials and rooming houses for all?

These fast-paced changes point at the potential to improve housing options. But there are also other, more ominous trends on the horizon. Companies can harness big data to find, renovate, and flip undervalued properties, all the while raising average housing prices and sharing few profits with the local economy. Institutional investors are buying up single-family housing, developing portfolios of thousands of properties, and engaging in price-fixing. While these efforts are likely to be bigger contributors to gentrification than new development—and, unlike new development, do not need to undergo any kind of vetting process—they are seeing less resistance than new construction in many of the cities facing housing shortages.

We can't possibly predict the shake-ups to come in the next decade. It is up to us to harness that change for good.

ACKNOWLEDGMENTS

Thank you to Zoë Pagnamenta, Alison Lewis, Katy O'Donnell, Remy Cawley, Elizabeth Dana, Melissa Veronesi, and Pete Beatty for improving this book and shepherding it into the world.

I'm indebted to each and every one of my sources for sharing their lives and homes with me—this book is obviously not possible without them. Thank you to Elizabeth Greenspan for inspiring me to pitch this book in the first place. Andrew Blum, Daniel Brook, Whitney Peeling, and Jo Piazza for publishing advice and companionship. Alex Baca for thoughtful feedback. Rachel Somerstein and Susan Levine for insights and confidence. My parents for sharing with me a love of books and architecture.

Writing a book while raising two young kids and holding down a full-time job (partly during a pandemic) was not easy. Thank you to Greg Heller for making it possible. Wherever and however we live, may it always be together.

NOTES

INTRODUCTION

1. Jonathan Tannen, "Philadelphia Housing Prices Are Up 22% in the Last 12 Months," EConsult Solutions, May 19, 2017, https://econsultso lutions.com/may-2017-philadelphia-housing-index-update/.

2. Brandon Cornett, "Is 2020 the Year Seattle's Housing Market Starts Rising Again?," Home Buying Institute, January 3, 2020, www.home buyinginstitute.com/news/will-seattle-start-rising-again/.

3. Alexander Hermann, "Price-to-Income Ratios Are Nearing Historic Highs," Joint Center for Housing Studies, September 13, 2018, www.jchs .harvard.edu/blog/price-to-income-ratios-are-nearing-historic-highs/.

4. Joint Center for Housing Studies, *The State of the Nation's Housing 2019* (Cambridge, MA: Harvard University, 2019), www.jchs.harvard .edu/state-nations-housing-2019.

5. Tom Mesenbourg, "A Look at the 1940 Census" (PowerPoint presentation for C-SPAN's *Washington Journal*, published by US Census Bureau, March 30, 2012), www.census.gov/newsroom/cspan/1940census /CSPAN_1940slides.pdf.

6. US Census Bureau, "Quarterly Residential Vacancies and Homeownership, Fourth Quarter 2019," news release no. CB20-05, January 30, 2020, www.census.gov/housing/hvs/files/currenthvspress.pdf.

7. Alanna McCargo and Sarah Strochak, "Mapping the Black Homeownership Gap," *Urban Wire* (blog), Urban Institute, February 26, 2018, www.urban.org/urban-wire/mapping-black-homeownership-gap.

8. Janelle Downing, "The Health Effects of the Foreclosure Crisis and Unaffordable Housing: A Systematic Review and Explanation of

Evidence," *Social Science & Medicine* 162 (2016): 88–96, www.sciencedi
rect.com/science/article/abs/pii/S0277953616302957.

9. Katherine A. Fowler et al., "Increase in Suicides Associated with
Home Eviction and Foreclosure During the US Housing Crisis: Findings from 16 National Violent Death Reporting System States, 2005–
2010," *American Journal of Public Health* 105 (2015): 311–316, https://doi
.org/10.2105/AJPH.2014.301945.

10. *National Healthcare Quality and Disparities Report: Chartbook on Rural
Health Care* (Rockville, MD: Agency for Healthcare Research and Quality,
2017), www.ahrq.gov/sites/default/files/wysiwyg/research/findings/nhqrdr
/chartbooks/qdr-ruralhealthchartbook-update.pdf.

11. J. Holt-Lunstad et al., "Loneliness and Social Isolation as Risk Factors for Mortality: A Meta-Analytic Review," *Perspectives on Psychological Science* 10, no. 2 (2015): 227–237, https://doi.org/10.1177/1745691614568352.

12. Lea Winerman, "By the Numbers: Antidepressants Use on the Rise,"
Monitor on Psychology, November 2017, www.apa.org/monitor/2017/11
/numbers.

13. "Achievements in Public Health, 1900–1999: Family Planning,"
Centers for Disease Control and Prevention, December 3, 1999, www.cdc
.gov/mmwr/preview/mmwrhtml/mm4847a1.htm.

14. William H. Frey, "The US Will Become 'Minority White,' in
2045, Census Projects," Brookings Institution, March 14, 2018, www
.brookings.edu/blog/the-avenue/2018/03/14/the-us-will-become
-minority-white-in-2045-census-projects/.

15. US Census Bureau, "Figure MS-2: Median Age at First Marriage:
1890 to Present," chart, www.census.gov/content/dam/Census/library
/visualizations/time-series/demo/families-and-households/ms-2.pdf.

16. Sally C. Curtin and Paul D. Sutton, "Marriage Rates in the United
States, 1900–2018," National Center for Health Statistics, last updated
April 29, 2020, www.cdc.gov/nchs/data/hestat/marriage_rate_2018/mar
riage_rate_2018.htm.

17. "Marriage & Divorce," American Psychological Association, www
.apa.org/topics/divorce/.

18. Erin Duffin, "Average Number of People per Family in the United
States from 1960 to 2019," chart, Statista, November 28, 2019, www.statista
.com/statistics/183657/average-size-of-a-family-in-the-us/; *2019 Profile of
Home Buyers and Sellers* (Washington, DC: National Association of Realtors,
2019), www.nysar.com/wp-content/uploads/2020/01/2019-NAR-HBS.pdf.

19. US Census Bureau, "U.S. Census Bureau Releases 2018 Families and Living Arrangements Tables," news release no. CB18-TPS.54, November 14, 2018, www.census.gov/newsroom/press-releases/2018/families.html.

20. "Life Expectancy," National Center for Health Statistics, last updated March 17, 2017, www.cdc.gov/nchs/fastats/life-expectancy.htm.

21. Richard Fry, "U.S. Women Near Milestone in the College-Educated Labor Force," *FactTank* (blog), Pew Research Center, June 20, 2019, www.pewresearch.org/fact-tank/2019/06/20/u-s-women-near-milestone-in-the-college-educated-labor-force/.

22. "Freelancing in America 2019," UpWork, www.upwork.com/i/freelancing-in-america/2019/.

23. Land Use: Zoning 2015–2016, California S.B. 1069, 2016, https://leginfo.legislature.ca.gov/faces/billTextClient.xhtml?bill_id=201520160SB1069; Land Use: Housing: 2nd Units 2015–2016, California A.B. 2299, 2016, https://leginfo.legislature.ca.gov/faces/billNavClient.xhtml?bill_id=201520160AB2299.

24. Health Research and Educational Trust, *Housing and the Role of Hospitals* (Chicago: American Hospital Association, 2017), www.hpoe.org/Reports-HPOE/2017/housing-role-of-hospitals.pdf.

25. Jennifer M. Ortman, Victoria A. Velkoff, and Howard Hogan, *An Aging Nation: The Older Population in the United States* (Washington, DC: US Census Bureau, 2014), www.census.gov/prod/2014pubs/p25-1140.pdf.

CHAPTER ONE

1. Keith Krawczynski, *Daily Life in the Colonial City* (Santa Barbara, CA: Greenwood, 2012), 323.

2. Carl Bridenbaugh, *Cities in the Wilderness: The First Century of Urban Life in America* (Oxford: Oxford University Press, 1971), 109.

3. Steven Ruggles, "The Decline of Intergenerational Coresidence in the United States, 1850 to 2000," *American Sociological Review* 72 (2007), http://users.hist.umn.edu/~ruggles/Articles/ASR-2007.pdf.

4. Bridenbaugh, *Cities in the Wilderness*, 151.

5. Krawczynski, *Daily Life*, 331.

6. Krawczynski, *Daily Life*, 336.

7. Wendy Gamber, *The Boardinghouse in Nineteenth-Century America* (Baltimore, MD: Johns Hopkins University Press, 2007).

8. "U.S. Population, 1790–2000: Always Growing," United States History, www.u-s-history.com/pages/h980.html.

9. Wikipedia, s.v. "1800 United States Census," last edited February 6, 2020, https://en.wikipedia.org/wiki/1800_United_States_Census.

10. "Immigration Timeline," Statue of Liberty–Ellis Island Foundation, Inc., www.libertyellisfoundation.org/immigration-timeline#1790.

11. Quoted in Jessica Leigh Hester, "A Brief History of Co-Living Spaces," *CityLab*, www.bloomberg.com/news/articles/2016-02-22/a-brief-history-of-co-living-spaces-from-19th-century-boarding-houses-to-millennial-compounds.

12. "Franklin Court," Independence National Historical Park Pennsylvania, National Park Service, last updated May 23, 2017, www.nps.gov/inde/learn/historyculture/places-franklincourt.htm.

13. Gamber, *The Boardinghouse*, 37.

14. Gamber, *The Boardinghouse*, 60.

15. Gamber, *The Boardinghouse*, 1–2.

16. Charles Dickens, *American Notes, Pictures from Italy, and a Child's History of England* (London: Chapman and Hall, Limited, 1891), 22.

17. Gwendolyn Wright, *Building the Dream: A Social History of Housing in America* (New York: Pantheon Books, 1981), 94.

18. Wright, *Building the Dream*, 139.

19. Joshua S. Yang, "The Anti-Chinese Cubic Air Ordinance," *American Journal of Public Health* 99, no. 3 (March 2009): 440, https://doi.org/10.2105/AJPH.2008.145813.

20. Wright, *Building the Dream*, 145.

21. Reverend Henry F. Cope, "The Conservation of the Modern Home," in *The Child Welfare Manual* (New York: University Society, 1915), 1:21.

22. Robert Bruegmann, *Sprawl: A Compact History* (Chicago: University of Chicago Press, 2005), 27.

23. Bruegmann, *Sprawl*, 27.

24. Wright, *Building the Dream*, 131.

25. Wright, *Building the Dream*, 195.

26. Wright, *Building the Dream*, 173.

CHAPTER TWO

1. Vincent J. Cannato, "A Home of One's Own," *National Affairs* 43 (Spring 2020), www.nationalaffairs.com/publications/detail/a-home-of-ones-own.

2. "Guide to People, Organizations, and Topics in *Prosperity and Thrift*," *Prosperity and Thrift: The Coolidge Era and the Consumer Economy,*

1921–1929, online exhibition, Library of Congress, https://memory.loc .gov/ammem/coolhtml/coolenab.html.

3. Mrs. W. B. Meloney, *Better Homes in America: Plan Book for Demonstration Week October 9 to 14, 1922* (1922, Project Gutenberg 2005), www .archive.org/stream/betterhomesiname07992gut/btrha10.txt.

4. Herbert Hoover, "The Home as an Investment," *The Delineator*, October 1922, 17.

5. LeeAnn Lands, "Be a Patriot, Buy a Home: Re-imagining Home Owners and Home Ownership in Early 20th Century Atlanta," *Journal of Social History* 41, no. 4 (2008): 943, https://go.gale.com/ps/anonymous?id= GALE%7CA181087047&sid=googleScholar&v=2.1&it=r&linkac cess=abs&issn=00224529&p=AONE&sw=w.

6. Kenneth Whyte, *Hoover: An Extraordinary Life in Extraordinary Times* (New York: Knopf, 2017), 274.

7. Richard Rothstein, *The Color of Law: A Forgotten History of How Our Government Segregated America* (New York: Liveright, 2017), 51.

8. Rothstein, *Color of Law*, 52.

9. Rothstein, *Color of Law*, 52.

10. Bruegmann, *Sprawl*, 36.

11. Hoover, "Home as an Investment," 91.

12. Wright, *Building the Dream*, 195.

13. Roger Lowenstein, "Who Needs the Mortgage-Interest Deduction?," *New York Times*, March 5, 2006, www.nytimes.com/2006/03/05 /magazine/who-needs-the-mortgageinterest-deduction.html.

14. Brian J. McCabe, *No Place Like Home: Wealth, Community and the Politics of Homeownership* (New York: Oxford University Press, 2016), 48.

15. Wright, *Building the Dream*, 222.

16. Wright, *Building the Dream*, 223.

17. Wright, *Building the Dream*, 227.

18. Wright, *Building the Dream*, 227.

19. Eugenie L. Birch, "The Housing and Slum Clearance Act and Its Effects on the Urban Planning Profession" (paper presented at Fannie Mae Conference on the Legacy of the 1949 Housing Act, October 1999), http://repository.upenn.edu/cplan_papers/26.

20. Matthew Chambers, Carlos Garriga, and Don E. Schlagenhauf, "Did Housing Policies Cause the Postwar Boom in Homeownership?," in *Housing and Mortgage Markets in Historical Perspective*, ed. Eugene N. White, Kenneth Snowden, and Price Fishback (Chicago: University of Chicago Press, 2014).

21. Bruegmann, *Sprawl*, 43.

22. Wright, *Building the Dream*, 260.

23. McCabe, *No Place Like Home*, 57.

24. David J. Erickson, *Housing Policy Revolution: Networks and Neighborhoods* (Washington, DC: Urban Institute Press, 2009), xiv.

25. John D. Landis, *Raising the Roof: California Housing Development Projections and Constraints, 1997–2020* (Sacramento: California Department of Housing and Urban Development, 2000), https://escholarship .org/uc/item/1391n947.

26. "Trends in New York City Housing Price Appreciation," in *State of New York City's Housing & Neighborhoods—2008 Report* (New York: Furman Center for Real Estate and Urban Policy, 2008), https://furman center.org/files/Trends_in_NYC_Housing_Price_Appreciation.pdf.

27. Alan Berube et al., *Finding Exurbia: America's Fast-Growing Communities at the Metropolitan Fringe* (Washington, DC: Brookings Institution, 2006), www.brookings.edu/research/finding-exurbia-americas-fast -growing-communities-at-the-metropolitan-fringe/.

28. US Census Bureau, "Homeownership Rate for the United States," Federal Reserve Bank of Saint Louis, accessed March 30, 2020, https:// fred.stlouisfed.org/series/RHORUSQ156N.

CHAPTER THREE

1. Dean Baker, *The Housing Bubble and the Great Recession: Ten Years Later* (Washington, DC: Center for Economic and Policy Research, 2018).

2. Alex F. Schwartz, *Housing Policy in the United States* (New York: Routledge, 2015), 411.

3. Dan Immergluck, *Preventing the Next Mortgage Crisis: The Meltdown, the Federal Response, and the Future of Housing in America* (New York: Rowman & Littlefield, 2015), 59.

4. *Neighborhood Stabilization Program: HUD and Grantees Are Taking Actions to Ensure Program Compliance but Data on Program Outputs Could Be Improved* (Washington, DC: US Government Accountability Office, 2010), www.gao.gov/assets/320/314145.pdf.

5. "Welcome to Invitation Homes," Invitation Homes, www.invita tionhomes.com/.

6. Ingrid Gould Ellen and Samuel Dastrup, *Housing and the Great Recession* (Stanford, CA: Stanford Center on Poverty and Inequality, 2012), https:// furmancenter.org/files/publications/HousingandtheGreatRecession.pdf.

7. Tommy Andres, "Divided Decade: How the Financial Crisis Changed Housing," *Marketplace*, December 17, 2018, www.marketplace.org/2018 /12/17/what-we-learned-housing/.

8. Michele Lerner, "10 Years Later: How the Housing Market Has Changed Since the Crash," *Washington Post*, October 4, 2018, www.wash ingtonpost.com/news/business/wp/2018/10/04/feature/10-years-later -how-the-housing-market-has-changed-since-the-crash.

9. *Millennial Generation: Information on the Economic Status of Millennial Households Compared to Previous Generations* (Washington, DC: US Government Accountability Office, 2019), www.gao.gov/products/GAO-20-194.

10. Goldman Sachs, "Millennials: Coming of Age," infographic, accessed March 30, 2020, www.goldmansachs.com/insights/archive/millennials/.

11. Jamie Ballard, "Millennials Are the Loneliest Generation," YouGov, July 30, 2019, https://today.yougov.com/topics/lifestyle/articles-reports /2019/07/30/loneliness-friendship-new-friends-poll-survey; Kate Julian, "Why Are Young People Having So Little Sex?," *The Atlantic*, December 2018, www.theatlantic.com/magazine/archive/2018/12/the-sex-recession /573949/.

12. Annie Nova, "Here's Why Millions of Millennials Are Not Homeowners," CNBC, August 30, 2019, www.cnbc.com/2019/08/30 /homeownership-eludes-millions-of-millennials-heres-why.html.

13. Nova, "Here's Why Millions."

14. "The Roots of the Crisis," Homelessness Response, Seattle.gov, accessed March 30, 2020, www.seattle.gov/homelessness/the-roots-of-the-crisis.

15. Antonio Bento et al., "Housing Market Effects of Inclusionary Zoning," *Cityscape* 11, no. 2 (2009): 7–26, www.jstor.org/stable/20868701.

16. Dan Bertolet and Nisma Gabobe, "LA ADU Story: How a State Law Sent Granny Flats off the Charts," Sightline Institute, April 5, 2019, www.sightline.org/2019/04/05/la-adu-story-how-a-state-law-sent -granny-flats-off-the-charts/.

17. Wikipedia, s.v. "YIMBY," last edited March 27, 2020, https:// en.wikipedia.org/wiki/YIMBY.

18. Diana Olick, "Foreign Purchases of American Homes Plunge 36% as Chinese Buyers Flee the Market," CNBC, July 17, 2019, www .cnbc.com/2019/07/17/foreign-purchases-of-american-homes-plunge -36percent-as-chinese-buyers-flee.html.

CHAPTER FOUR

1. Benedict Carey, "Families' Every Fuss, Archived and Analyzed," *New York Times*, May 22, 2010, www.nytimes.com/2010/05/23/science /23family.html.

2. Debra Umberson and Jennifer Karas Montez, "Social Relationships and Health: A Flashpoint for Health Policy," *Journal of Health and Social Behavior* 51 (2010): S54–S66, https://doi.org/10.1177/0022146510383501.

3. Umberson and Montez, "Social Relationships."

4. Frank Hobbs and Nicole Stoops, *Demographic Trends in the 20th Century* (Washington, DC: US Census Bureau, 2002), 141.

5. US Census Bureau, "Millennials Outnumber Baby Boomers, and Are Far More Diverse, Census Bureau Reports," June 25, 2015, www.cen sus.gov/newsroom/press-releases/2015/cb15-113.html.

6. US Census Bureau, "Quarterly Residential Vacancies and Home-ownership," www.census.gov/housing/hvs/files/currenthvspress.pdf.

7. Andrew Arenge, Stephanie Perry, and Ashley Tallevi, "Poll: Majority of Millennials Are in Debt, Hitting Pause on Major Life Events," NBC, April 4, 2018, www.nbcnews.com/news/us-news/poll-majority -millennials-are-debt-hitting-pause-major-life-events-n862376.

8. Tim Henderson, "For Many Millennials, Marriage Can Wait," *Stateline* (blog), Pew Charitable Trusts, December 20, 2016, www.pewtrusts .org/en/research-and-analysis/blogs/stateline/2016/12/20/for-many -millennials-marriage-can-wait.

9. "Chapter 2: Housing Maintenance Code," TenantNet, accessed March 30, 2020, http://tenant.net/Other_Laws/HMC/sub3/art4.html.

10. Cigna, "New Cigna Study Reveals Loneliness at Epidemic Levels in America," news release, May 1, 2018, www.cigna.com/newsroom/news -releases/2018/new-cigna-study-reveals-loneliness-at-epidemic-levels-in -america.

CHAPTER FIVE

1. Jake Blumgart, "How Bernie Sanders Made Burlington Affordable," *Slate*, January 19, 2016, https://slate.com/business/2016/01/bernie-sanders -made-burlingtons-land-trust-possible-its-still-an-innovative-and -effective-model-of-affordable-housing-today.html.

2. "Customizable Tiny Home," Allswell, accessed March 30, 2020, https://allswellhome.com/pages/buythehome.

3. Mark J. Perry, "New US Homes Today Are 1,000 Square Feet Larger Than in 1973 and Living Space per Person Has Nearly Doubled," American Enterprise Institute, June 5, 2016, www.aei.org/carpe-diem /new-us-homes-today-are-1000-square-feet-larger-than-in-1973-and -living-space-per-person-has-nearly-doubled/.

4. Natalia Siniavskaia, "Lot Size Remains Record Low," *Eye on Housing*, August 31, 2018, http://eyeonhousing.org/2018/08/lot-size-remains -record-low/.

5. Rose Quint, "Tiny Homes Might Have Potential Buyers," *Eye on Housing*, February 7, 2018, http://eyeonhousing.org/2018/02/tiny-homes -might-have-potential-buyers/.

6. Ralph McLaughlin, "Americans (Can't Get No) Home Size Satisfaction," Trulia, March 1, 2017, www.trulia.com/research/home-size -survey-march-16/.

7. "San Francisco, CA Rental Market Trends," RENTCafé, accessed March 30, 2020, www.rentcafe.com/average-rent-market-trends/us/ca/san -francisco/.

8. Patrick McGregor, "Do Tiny Homes Live Up to the Hype?," PropertyShark, February 11, 2019, www.propertyshark.com/Real-Estate -Reports/2019/02/11/do-tiny-homes-live-up-to-the-hype/.

9. *2017 Manufactured Housing Facts: Industry Overview* (Arlington, VA: Manufactured Housing Institute, 2017), www.manufacturedhousing .org/wp-content/uploads/2017/10/2017-MHI-Quick-Facts.pdf.

10. *California's Future: Housing* (San Francisco: Public Policy Institute of California, 2018), www.ppic.org/wp-content/uploads/r-118hjr.pdf.

11. *2019 California Housing Profile* (Washington, DC: National Low Income Housing Coalition, 2019), https://nlihc.org/sites/default/files /SHP_CA.pdf.

12. Sam Morgen, "City and County Step Up Efforts to Battle Homelessness as Numbers Rise," *Bakersfield Californian*, March 20, 2019, www.bakersfield.com/news/city-and-county-step-up-efforts-to-battle -homelessness-as/article_936b9b74-4b6a-11e9-922c-a341247ce397.html.

13. Los Angeles Homeless Services Authority, "Greater Los Angeles Homeless Count Shows 12% Rise in Homelessness," news release, June 4, 2019, www.lahsa.org/news?article=558-greater-los-angeles-homeless -count-shows-12-rise-in-homelessness.

14. Bertolet and Gabobe, "LA ADU Story."

15. Krystal Navar, "ADUs in LA's Housing Progress Report," *ADU Blog*, Modative, January 9, 2019, www.modative.com/adu-blog/los-angeles-adu-housing-report-2018.

16. Salma Nurmohamed, "Vancouver's Laneway Love-In: Little Homes, Big Success," CBC, November 5, 2016, www.cbc.ca/news/canada/british-columbia/laneway-vancouver-coachhouse-density-1.3835335.

17. Wikipedia, s.v. "Sears Modern Homes," last edited March 1, 2020, https://en.wikipedia.org/wiki/Sears_Modern_Homes.

18. Anne Brown, Donald Shoup, and Vinit Mukhija, "How Single-Family Garages Can Ease California's Housing Crisis," *CityLab*, April 19, 2019, www.citylab.com/perspective/2019/04/convert-garage-apartments-affordable-housing-crisis-adu/587434/.

19. Julie Lasky, "The Enduring Appeal of Micro Living," *New York Times*, September 3, 2019, www.nytimes.com/2019/09/03/realestate/the-enduring-appeal-of-micro-living.html.

20. *Pushed Out: Housing Displacement in an Unaffordable Region* (New York: Regional Plan Association, 2017), http://library.rpa.org/pdf/RPA-Pushed-Out-Housing-Displacement-in-an-Unaffordable-Region.pdf.

CHAPTER SIX

1. "Two-to-Four Unit Buildings in Cook County's Rental Market," Institute for Housing Studies at DePaul University, June 13, 2012, www.housingstudies.org/releases/two-four-unit-buildings-cook-countys-rental-market/.

2. P. Muennig, B. Jiao, and E. Singer, "Living with Parents or Grandparents Increases Social Capital and Survival: 2014 General Social Survey—National Death Index," *SSM—Population Health* 4 (2017):71–75, https://doi.org/10.1016/j.ssmph.2017.11.001.

3. "Multigenerational Households," Generations United, accessed March 30, 2020, www.gu.org/explore-our-topics/multigenerational-households/.

4. D'Vera Cohn and Jeffrey S. Passel, "A Record 64 Million Americans Live in Multigenerational Households," *Fact Tank* (blog), Pew Research Center, April 5, 2018, https://www.pewresearch.org/fact-tank/2018/04/05/a-record-64-million-americans-live-in-multigenerational-households/.

5. Richard Fry, "The Number of People in the Average U.S. Household Is Going Up for the First Time in over 160 Years," *Fact Tank* (blog), Pew Research Center, October 1, 2019, www.pewresearch.org/fact-tank

/2019/10/01/the-number-of-people-in-the-average-u-s-household-is-going-up-for-the-first-time-in-over-160-years/.

6. Steven Ruggles, "Multigenerational Families in Nineteenth-Century America," *Continuity and Change* 18, no. 1 (2003): 139–165, http://doi.org/10.1017/S0268416003004466.

7. Ruggles, "Multigenerational Families."

8. Steven Ruggles, "The Decline of Intergenerational Coresidence in the United States, 1850 to 2000," *American Sociological Review* 72, no. 6 (2007): 964–989, http://doi.org/10.1177/000312240707200606.

9. Ruggles, "Multigenerational Families."

10. Ruggles, "Decline of Intergenerational Coresidence."

11. Cohn and Passel, "A Record 64 Million Americans."

12. P. K., "Historical Home Prices: Monthly Median Value in the US from 1953–2019," *DQYDJ*, October 3, 2019, https://dqydj.com/historical-home-prices/.

13. Jeanne Batalova, Brittany Blizzard, and Jessica Bolter, "Frequently Requested Statistics on Immigrants and Immigration in the United States," Migration Policy Institute, February 14, 2020, www.migrationpolicy.org/article/frequently-requested-statistics-immigrants-and-immigration-united-states.

14. Mitra Toossi, "A Century of Change: The U.S. Labor Force, 1950–2050," *Monthly Labor Review* (May 2002), www.bls.gov/opub/mlr/2002/05/art2full.pdf.

15. Mitra Toossi and Teresa L. Morisi, *Women in the Workforce Before, During, and After the Great Recession* (Washington, DC: US Bureau of Labor Statistics, 2017), www.bls.gov/spotlight/2017/women-in-the-workforce-before-during-and-after-the-great-recession/pdf/women-in-the-workforce-before-during-and-after-the-great-recession.pdf.

16. Natasha V. Pilkauskas and Christina Cross, "Beyond the Nuclear Family: Trends in Children Living in Shared Households," *Demography* 55 (2018): 2283–2297, https://doi.org/10.1007/s13524-018-0719-y.

17. Cohn and Passel, "A Record 64 Million Americans."

18. Cohn and Passel, "A Record 64 Million Americans."

19. *Parents and the High Cost of Child Care: 2015 Report* (Arlington, VA: Child Care Aware America, 2015), www.childcareaware.org/wp-content/uploads/2016/05/Parents-and-the-High-Cost-of-Child-Care-2015-FINAL.pdf.

20. Derek Thompson, "Why Child Care Is So Ridiculously Expensive," *The Atlantic*, November 26, 2019, www.theatlantic.com/ideas/archive/2019/11/why-child-care-so-expensive/602599/.

21. Cohn and Passel, "A Record 64 Million Americans."

22. Muennig, Jiao, and Singer, "Living with Parents."

23. Muennig, Jiao, and Singer, "Living with Parents."

24. "Living With/Near Parents or Child," CFP Housing Grants, Housing & Development Board, accessed March 30, 2020, https://hdb.gov.sg/cs/infoweb/residential/buying-a-flat/resale/living-with-near-parents-or-married-child.

25. Stephanie Firestone, "Incentivizing Multigenerational Living," *Thinking Policy* (blog), AARP, May 23, 2019, https://blog.aarp.org/thinking-policy/incentivizing-multigenerational-living.

26. Julia Schnatz, "Mehrgenerationenhäuser II in Germany," Centre for Public Impact, August 3, 2018, www.centreforpublicimpact.org/case-study/mehrgenerationenhauser-germany/.

27. "Grandfamilies," Generations United, accessed March 30, 2020, www.gu.org/explore-our-topics/grandfamilies/.

28. Peter Uhlenberg and Jenny De Jong Gierveld, "Age-Segregation in Later Life: An Examination of Personal Networks," *Ageing & Society* 24, no. 1 (2004): 5–28, https://doi.org/10.1017/S0144686X0300151X.

29. *AARP 2018 Home and Community Preferences Survey: A National Survey of Adults Age 18-Plus* (Washington, DC: AARP, 2018), www.aarp.org/content/dam/aarp/research/surveys_statistics/liv-com/2018/home-community-preferences-survey.doi.10.26419-2Fres.00231.001.pdf.

30. Eli Spevak and Melissa Stanton, *The ABCs of ADUs* (Washington, DC: AARP, 2019), www.aarp.org/content/dam/aarp/livable-communities/livable-documents/documents-2019/ADU-guide-web-singles-071619.pdf.

31. "Meeting the Future Housing Needs of Seniors," PD&R Edge, HUD User, accessed March 30, 2020, www.huduser.gov/portal/pdredge/pdr-edge-featd-article-112017.html.

CHAPTER SEVEN

1. Anne Case and Angus Deaton, "Mortality and Morbidity in the 21st Century," *Brookings Papers on Economic Activity* (Spring 2017): 397–476.

2. John F. Helliwell, Richard Layard, and Jeffrey D. Sachs, *World Happiness Report 2019* (New York: Sustainable Development Solutions Network, 2019).

3. Ning Xia and Huige Li, "Loneliness, Social Isolation, and Cardiovascular Health," *Antioxidants & Redox Signaling* 28, no. 9 (2018): 837–851, http://doi.org/10.1089/ars.2017.7312.

4. Craig Hales et al., "Trends in Obesity and Severe Obesity Prevalence in US Youth and Adults by Sex and Age, 2007–2008 to 2015–2016," *Journal of the American Medical Association* 319, no. 16 (2018):1723–1725, http://doi.org/10.1001/jama.2018.3060.

5. Lauren Taylor, "Housing and Health: An Overview of the Literature," *Health Affairs*, June 7, 2018, www.healthaffairs.org/do/10.1377/hpb20180313.396577/full/.

6. Enterprise, "Affordable Housing Reduces Medicaid Costs, New Report Shows," news release, February 25, 2016, www.enterprisecommunity.org/news-and-events/news-releases/affordable-housing-reduces-medicaid-costs.

7. Tama Leventhal and Jeanne Brooks-Gunn, "Moving to Opportunity: An Experimental Study of Neighborhood Effects on Mental Health," *American Journal of Public Health* 93, no. 9 (2003): 1576–1582, http://doi.org/10.2105/ajph.93.9.1576.

8. "Transcript and Analysis: California Gov. Gavin Newsom's 2020 State of the State," Capital Public Radio, February 19, 2020, www.capradio.org/articles/2020/02/19/transcript-and-analysis-california-gov-gavin-newsoms-2020-state-of-the-state/.

9. "Health Action Plan," Enterprise, www.enterprisecommunity.org/solutions-and-innovation/health-and-housing/affordable-housing-designed-for-health/health-action-plan.

10. Children's Hospital of Philadelphia, "Children's Hospital of Philadelphia Expands Community Asthma Prevention Program in Partnership with Philadelphia Housing Development Corporation," news release, December 17, 2018, www.chop.edu/news/children-s-hospital-philadelphia-expands-community-asthma-prevention-program-partnership.

11. DMC: Destination Medical Center, https://dmc.mn/.

12. Harvest, www.harvestbyhillwood.com/.

13. Gillian M. Sandstrom and Elizabeth W. Dunn, "Social Interactions and Well-Being: The Surprising Power of Weak Ties," *Personality and Social Psychology Bulletin* 40, no. 7 (2014): 910–922, https://doi.org/10.1177/0146167214529799.

CHAPTER EIGHT

1. Gina Kolata, "What Made New York So Hospitable for Coronavirus?," *New York Times*, March 26, 2020, www.nytimes.com/2020/03/26 /health/coronavirus-nyc-spread.html.

2. Indermit Gill, "Coronavirus Lessons from New York and San Francisco," Brookings Institution, April 7, 2020, www.brookings.edu /blog/future-development/2020/04/07/coronavirus-lessons-from-new -york-and-san-francisco/.

3. C. J. Hughes, "Coronavirus Escape: To the Suburbs," *New York Times*, May 8, 2020, www.nytimes.com/2020/05/08/realestate/coronavirus-escape -city-to-suburbs.html.

4. Joseph Pimentel, "Californians in Cramped Quarantine Are Eyeing Building 'Granny Flats,'" Bisnow, March 26, 2020, www.bisnow .com/los-angeles/news/multifamily/expect-adus-to-be-on-the-rise-in -california-103600.

5. Jon Dishotsky (@JonDishotsky), "For members that are sheltering in place, 'It's a lot more fun to be cooped up with your friends than isolated in a lonely apartment,'" Twitter, March 30, 2020, 6:30 p.m., https://twitter .com/JonDishotsky/status/1244663178815885312.

6. Anita Hofschneider, "This Hawaii Multi-Generational Family of 7 Worries as Coronavirus Spreads," *Honolulu Civil Beat*, March 26, 2020, www.civilbeat.org/2020/03/this-hawaii-multi-generational-family-of -7-worries-as-coronavirus-spreads/.

7. Ruth Kogen Goodwin, "I'm Sheltering in Place with My In-Laws… and It's Actually Amazing. Here's Why," *HuffPost*, April 25, 2020, www.huffpost.com/entry/covid-19-shelter-in-place-in-laws_n_5ea 198b9c5b69150246e998f.

8. Kai Chen, Meng Wang, Conghong Huang, Patrick L. Kinney, and Anastas T. Paul, "Air Pollution Reduction and Mortality Benefit during the COVID-19 Outbreak in China," *The Lancet Planetary Health* 4, no. 6 (2020): e210–e212, https://doi: 10.1016/S2542-5196(20)30107-8.

9. Richard D. Kahlenberg, "How Minneapolis Ended Single-Family Zoning," Century Foundation, October 24, 2019, https://tcf.org/content /report/minneapolis-ended-single-family-zoning/.

10. Cody Nelson, "Map: Black Homeownership Rates in Twin Cities Are Among the Lowest in the U.S.," MPR News, December 20, 2018, www.mprnews.org/story/2018/12/20/research-lab-black-homeownership.

11. Clare Duffy, "Zillow Wants to Keep Cashing In on Flipping Homes, but First It Needs to Stop Losing Money," CNN, August 7, 2019, www.cnn .com/2019/08/07/tech/zillow-earnings-flipping/index.html.

12. Matthew Desmond, "How Homeownership Became the Engine of American Inequality," *New York Times Magazine*, May 9, 2017, www .nytimes.com/2017/05/09/magazine/how-homeownership-became-the -engine-of-american-inequality.html.

13. Raleigh Norris, "Common Reveals Atlanta Coliving Expansion Plans in Partnership with Domos," Common, September 9, 2019, www.common.com/blog/2019/09/common-reveals-atlanta-coliving -expansion-plans-in-partnership-with-domos/.

14. Michael J. Rosenfeld, Reuben J. Thomas, and Sonia Hausen, "Disintermediating Your Friends: How Online Dating in the United States Displaces Other Ways of Meeting," *Proceedings of the National Academy of Sciences of the United States of America* 116, no. 36 (2019): 17753–17758, http://doi.org//10.1073/pnas.1908630116.

15. "Who Lives in Federally Assisted Housing?," National Low Income Housing Coalition, November 2012, https://nlihc.org/sites/default /files/HousingSpotlight2-2.pdf.

INDEX

COLIN M. LENTON

DIANA LIND is an urban policy specialist whose writing has appeared in the *New York Times*, the *Philadelphia Inquirer*, *Architectural Record*, and *Next City*, where she also served as Editor in Chief and Executive Director. She is a housing fellow for the international nonprofit NewCities and lives in Philadelphia.